PRAISE for

Achieving NO LIMITS—Embracing Change

"Al Foxx is a powerful, courageous and honest author who takes you through an incredible and inspiring journey of self-discovery and leaves you with a feeling of gratitude and self-awareness. Foxx's book *Achieving NO LIMITS-Embracing Change* is insightful, educational and a must read! It is filled with valuable life lessons without being preachy. Foxx shares his life story and nuggets of wisdom about things we take for granted every day, in a way that only someone with his experience could share.

One of my favorite quotes by Foxx is: 'Choices are the most powerful freedom we have.... our attitudes will either make us or break us. One attitude at a time, we're either building a castle or a coffin. Your attitude is your choice.' He has learned to face the calamities in his life with courage and gratitude.

Achieving NO LIMITS-Embracing Change describes how Foxx reached self-acceptance and became a humble and gracious man as a result of becoming a positive person. *Achieving NO LIMITS- Embracing Change* is moving, inspiring and unforgettable--the kind of book you want to read with a hi-lighter!"   **--Shirin Sherkat, Psy.D.**
Parent Strategist, Author & Founder of *Create Happy Kids*
www.CreateHappyKids.com

"The story of Al Foxx's life and what he has had to endure is incredible. He went from a happy go lucky 18-year old to a 19-year old with a broken body in one moment. But his spirit was not damaged. Despite this terribly devastating accident, he has risen and surpassed all of the doctor's predictions of his future life. Not only is he a great writer, but his speeches are wonderfully humorous. Al Foxx has a unique ability to turn his pain into humor. *Achieving NO LIMITS-Embracing Change* is a must read for anyone suffering from any kind of limitation in their life."

--Bruce Raine
Author of *Attitude Determines Destiny*
www.BruceRaine.com/Author/Bruce-Raine/

"Oh-my-gosh, I can do it! *Achieving NO LIMITS-Embracing Change* took the limits off my own life and gave me hope that I have a future after all."

--Kelly Clark, Wife, Mother and Head Injury Survivor

"I found Al's book, *Achieving NO LIMITS, Embracing Change* to be a great read for anyone facing challenges."

--Matthew Krings, PT, MPT, OCS
Apple Physical Therapy, Kirkland, WA
www.ApplePT.com/kirkland

"I really believed and thought I knew what it meant to 'NEVER QUIT' until I read *Achieving NO LIMITS, Embracing Change* by Al Foxx. Al's story of struggle through challenges and his eventual victory will inspire you like never before as you realize what true perseverance is and how to toss away the limiting beliefs society and we ourselves place on our shoulders. Choosing to accept responsibility for the abilities you do have is the path to success. Thank you, Al, for offering so many life lessons from your incredible life that people from all walks of life can relate to."

--Karen Szillat
Early Childhood Professional &
Author of *Empowering the Children:*
12 Universal Values Your Child Must Learn to Succeed in Life
www.EmpoweringtheChildren.com

"Al Foxx tells his inspiring story with honesty and humility. I walked away from reading *Achieving NO LIMITS-Embracing Change* convinced that no matter what tragic events may happen my ability to react has no limits. I have the power to respond with acceptance, belief, and compassion. It's my choice."

--Michael Buschmohle
President of Applause Associates & International Speaker/Trainer

"*Achieving NO LIMITS-Embracing Change* is a true inspirational gift of hope for anyone who reads it. Foxx provides a faith born optimism that gives people the courage to not only dream big, but to realize their dreams. He is not a quitter and he provides some very basic and really quite simple life formulas that have big impact. For example, his presentation to *'focus on what you have, and not what you don't have'* actually changed my life. Another one he discusses is to *'focus on your progress, not toward the perfection you would like'*, yet another jewel of wisdom that touched me.

His humility and the joy and gratitude exhibited in his daily life are truly refreshing. I wish I could bottle it up! When reading this book, you'll realize he writes the way he speaks, from the heart. Mr. Foxx is truly authentic–the real deal."

--Bonnie Richter-Robinson
Executive Director, North Region EMS & Trauma Care Council

"Having both met Al Foxx personally and read his book *Achieving NO LIMITS-Embracing Change,* I highly respect him and thoroughly enjoyed his many stories of rehabilitation which included acceptance of his situation, believing he could write a happy ending and the importance of caring about other people. He proposes that learning adaptability skills can be used in all areas of your life. His story comes from a kind and warm heart, a definite 'feel good' book."

--Diana E. Ruiz
Author of *How to Use Your Mind, Body & Water Connection to Awake*
Your Inner Fountain of Youth
www.HealingYourLifeWithWater.com

"Al's book, *Achieving NO LIMITS-Embracing Change* is fresh and authentic. Al tells the story of what it is really like to have an unexpected event change your life forever. I found the book able to provide hope to anyone who has dealt with any kind of life crisis. I came away with a refreshed perspective and definitely with regained hope for those who experience challenges that seem impossible to overcome."

--Frank Reed,
Author of *In God We Trust Dollars & Sense*
www.SpundRetirementRadio.com

"Al Foxx throws out torches for your path in life and leads people through the darkness. *'Achieving NO LIMITS-Embracing Change'* showed me that a positive attitude combined with a healthy sense of humor is a winning formula to make your dreams come true."

--Terry Gargas, MS.
Retired Rehabilitation Counselor and Author of
Reinventing Yourself from the Inside Out

"Al Foxx naturally entertains and inspires with his words. Reading *Achieving NO LIMITS-Embracing Change* will provide wisdom gained from Al's personal experience with a life changing motorcycle accident.

He reinforces it with stories that make you understand how fast you can lose the life you always thought would be yours and the various stages you go through before you reclaim your life again."

--Joanna Cummings
Author of *Kick Butts Take Names*
www.KickButtsTakeNames.com/training/

"Achieving NO LIMITS-Embracing Change is truly refreshing book which will bring you into the world of people with disabilities. You will realize the isolation and harsh challenges, such as rejection, that people with disabilities face. Al's delightful attitude and his Winners Don't Quit approach have brought him out of that world. Now he shares how we can improve our relationships and make better connections with people with disabilities. Al has learned many of the ingredients needed to gain the support and respect of all those in his life. He is a delightful person and purposefully continues to work toward his goals, making the changes needed to be the best he can be!"

--H.C. Joe Raymond
Life Coach & Author of *Embracing Change from the Inside Out*
www.hcjoeraymond.com/

"Al Foxx showed me the inner strength people with disabilities have. After reading Achieving NO LIMITS—Embracing Change, I realize I have much more strength than I thought I had".   **--Leo Novsky**
Author of Speak with Power
www.SpeakWithPower.net

"We are always more resilient than we think. In his motivational and optimistic book, Al Foxx shows you how to face the unexpected and use what you've learned to be happier in life."

--Jag Randhawa
Author of *The Bright Idea Box*
Winner of Silver Medal in Axiom Business Book Awards
www.TheBrightIdeaBox.com

"It takes a remarkable person to make his dreams come true. It takes an even more of a remarkable person who has a disability to make his dreams come true. After reading *Achieving NO LIMITS—Embracing Change*, I believe I can achieve my dreams too. Thank you, Al."

--Heather Picket
Author of *Inside Secrets to a CEO's Mindset*

"*Achieving NO LIMITS-Embracing Change* helped me understand the challenges with disabilities; individuals who have lost all that they previously held dear and are now challenged to reinvent themselves. Now I better understand how much courage it takes to not let what others say or think of you, affect how you see yourself. *Achieving No Limits-Embracing Change* shows the reader that with the right attitude and fortitude, Winners Don't Quit!"   **--Earl Bell**
Author of *Winning in Baseball and Business*
www.WinningInbBaseballAndbBusiness.com

"I was amazed at Al Foxx's ability to recognize the many mentors he had in his life throughout his adversity and struggle through major changes. It makes me w3ant to become a mentor and help others in that way too. I would definitely recommend Al's book for anyone who wants to be inspired with the right attitude, the attitude of gratitude."
--Mike Margolis
Author of *The Athlete within You*
www.TheAthletewWithinyou

"I absolutely loved the way your book, *Achieving NO LIMITS- Embracing Change* identified with the problems I face every day. I was amazing! Good job. Thank you!"
--Amiko Conners, Head Injury Survivor

"Al Foxx teaches us how we can get through the pain more quickly and extract greater meaning from the nonnegotiable events of life."
Wanda Buckner
Author of *Choosing Energy Therapy:*
Improving the Lives of people and their Animals
http://www.HealingEnergyServices.com

"When reading *Achieving NO LIMITS-Embracing Change,* you will laugh, cry and be inspired by Al's journey in life. No matter what struggle or adversity you may face, Al Foxx's book is a must read."
Lori Tsugawa Whaley
Author of *The courage of a Samurai*

v

Hi Shanika,
Focus on what you have,
not what you don't have.

Al Fox

Achieving

NO LIMITS

Embracing Change

Winners Don't Quit!

Al Foxx 10-22-14

Founder, Winners Don't Quit Association

Motivational Humorist and Keynote Speaker

AVIVA
PUBLISHING
New York

Achieving NO LIMITS--Embracing Change

© 2014 by AL FOXX

ISBN#: 978-1-938686-02-3

Library of Congress Control Number: 2012944312

(Self Help/Inspirational/Disability)

Cover and Interior Book Design: Bonnie Richter

Editing: Michael Buschmohle, Mark Robertson, Bonnie Richter and Fritz Fuchs

Published by Aviva Publishing

Lake Placid, NY

518-523-1320

www.avivapubs.com

www.AchievingNoLimits.com

www.AttitudeMan.com, www.WinnersDontQuit.org

$19.95 per copy + 9.5 percent sales tax for orders in Washington State

To order this title by mail, please include price as noted above, $5.10 shipping for each book ordered. Send requests to:

Al Foxx, President of Winners Don't Quit Association

PO Box 2347, Woodinville, WA 98072

Website: www.WinnersDontQuitAssociation.com

Email: AlFoxx@AttitudeMan.com or AlFoxx@AlFoxx.com

DEDICATION

This **book is dedicated** to the many mentors and role models I have been blessed with throughout my life of rehabilitation. These individuals generously provided me knowledge, quality time, advice, and resources when I needed them.

Many were dedicated to help me set goals and to develop key contacts to further my ambitions toward a new career path after my life-changing motorcycle crash. Others have provided spiritual and life management guidance, motivation, emotional support, as well as role modeling.

Because these relationships came into my life, I have learned to trust, respect and value others, a key component to my eventual recovery from self-pity, self-absorption and isolation that resulted from my fear and poor attitude.

I have individually recognized each of these key people toward the end of this book in *Chapter 29*. Each person listed has provided many positive contributions (too many to list in the chapter) and many still continue to provide me the love, care and support we all need for happiness.

I know these individuals believe in me and want to see me succeed and I will not let them down. The driving internal force to be as successful as I can doesn't necessarily mean financial success. I define my success as becoming the best man I can be and helping others to be their best.

CONTENTS

FOREWORD

Imagine you are driving home from work and your car is broadsided by a truck. Your mangled body is thrown from the car and you suffer a severe head injury. After weeks in a coma, you awaken with brain damage and paralysis only to hear the surgeon tell your family, "I'm sorry, but he will never again talk, or walk, or be able to work or drive a car."

This is what happened to Al Foxx, except he was on a motorcycle when he crashed into a truck. He awoke from a coma in a vegetative state and the doctors proclaimed that his former life was over. But the doctors didn't know Al Foxx.

This book proves beyond doubt that there can be truly No Limits. Al Foxx's life story of trauma and recovery is inspiring. I've known Al for more than a dozen years and have found him to be a man of determination and faith who has fought through periods of loss and anger, depression and loneliness.

He is a gifted writer whose words flow from his heart. He's also an award-winning comedian who has learned to accept the life he has and not complain about what he doesn't have. After years of rehabilitation, he now generously shares his story with audiences across America and in Canada as an inspirational speaker.

This book is both a story and a tool for examining your own life. As Al says, "We've all had our own motorcycle crashes and had to recover."

These pages, filled with thought-provoking questions, are offered to help and heal. You will meet a man for all seasons whose life continues to offer hope and inspiration. And, as you'll happily discover, today Al Foxx talks, walks, works, and drives a car. Why? --Because there are truly No Limits.

Michael Buschmohle

President, Applause Associates

AUTHOR'S NOTE

THIS BOOK FULFILLS a dream of mine to inspire individuals to be hopeful about their lives and to look on the future positively and to see opportunity in challenges or unexpected change. Hope nurtures our lives like the rain. Without hope would we even get up in the morning?

The first part of this book is a story about an 18-year old teen (me), whose idyllic life was full of hope and then my life turned for a big change and was unexpectedly ripped apart by a motorcycle crash. The second part of the book focuses on my many struggle s to find hope again and to maintain hope during my rehabilitation and the many lessons I learned.

It was on May 7, 1980 that I jumped onto my powerful bike that carried me down country roads and busy city streets where I weaved between cars. I loved the freedom I felt when riding my Yamaha 650 Special. I felt invincible. I had it all. Life was amazing!

I knew I should slow down, but I kept speeding up. I never even saw the truck that came out of a side street, through the stop sign. I had the right-of-way, but his line of sight to the oncoming traffic was blocked, so he pulled out into the street thinking, or at least hoping, all would be well.

I suffered a massive traumatic brain injury that left me completely incapacitated. Emergency room surgeons said that even if I lived, I'd never be the same, that I'd be different, physically, emotionally and intellectually.

I had sustained a brain stem contusion, a ruptured spleen, broken facial bones and massive internal hemorrhaging. A tar-roofer by trade, my world collapsed when doctors told me I would never walk, talk or drive again.

What doctors didn't anticipate was the strength of my spirit. I was unwilling to accept the gloomy prognosis.

I learned that my state of mind dictated my experience of the world around me. If I had a hopeful outlook, it released me from a lot of pain. Therefore, if hoping that we will recover from an illness makes us feel calm and peaceful, then already we reduce the emotional and even physical pain that we feel and improve the quality of our experience for that moment.

However, if the odds are against recovery and you can find acceptance of your condition, then that too can bring peace of mind. Peace of mind means no stress, keeping us in a more relaxed state which can increase the chance of recovery. It is well documented that emotional well-being can be crucial to recovery from illness.

Most of us get stressed because we become attached to an outcome and we have an expectation of what we want to happen to make us happy. If that expectation is not met, then there is disappointment and in some cases depression. Who is the one that decides what a realistic expectation is? When do you decide that hope is fruitless and acceptance is the only option? It has to be the individual's choice – whatever choice brings them peace, is the right one for them.

In my opinion, hope is valid if there is a chance, however small, that something is possible. Hope can be a lifeline and who has the authority to decide when to take that lifeline away?

Today, nearly 34 years later, I know how to keep hope alive in my life. I have learned that hope is not wishful thinking. Hope is a state of mind that inspires me to help others. I have learned that hope is manifested when I'm helping others. I have learned that the more people I help the more hopeful I feel.

Hope by definition, is a feeling of expectation and desire for a positive outcome. In many cases, we cling most tightly to hope when something unexpected or undesirable occurs.

Hope and faith often go together. Hope is putting faith to work when doubting would be easier. Hope keeps something alive in us even when circumstances seem impossible. Hope is a dimension of the soul. Hope is an orientation of the spirit and the heart.

We have all experienced life-changing events where we cling to hope like it's our best friend. This book highlights what I had to ultimately learn about hope. These lessons are vital for everyone. My motorcycle crash didn't create the need for me to learn them; it just made it more obvious that I needed to learn them.

Hope motivates positive actions that will lead us to positive results. Hope is a natural stress reliever. Hope helps strengthen the immune system. Hope improves social relationships. And best of all, hope simply makes us happy.

Thank you for buying my book. My desire would be that you always have hope, regardless of the challenge.

ACKNOWLEDGEMENTS

THIS BOOK WAS INSPIRED by four very special and specific people in my life. Michael Buschmohle has been one of my most consistent and long-term mentors, hanging out with me for at least the past fifteen years. As a very well educated catholic priest who moved on to marry and build a new life, he understands what embracing change is all about. He has helped me in countless ways to organize my messages and has supported me to build my natural talents such as my sense of humor and writing skills.

Cheryl Peterson assisted me with my first book, *NO LIMITS*. Cheryl's organizational management skills were invaluable for me to get my start as an author. I will never forget to be grateful for her dedication to me and my dreams.

Bonnie Richter has believed in me and my mission for many years now and has helped me with developing, designing, editing, organizing and marketing my books. She has been an incredible content editor and I will always cherish our many conversations, sometimes debates about expanding and being clear regarding my message. Bonnie has spent countless hours working with me and listening to my many ideas and dreams. Her contributions and skills in detail and research have paved the way to my new book, *Achieving NO LIMITS-Embracing Change* and to continue to improve telling my story.

And last, had it not been for Patrick Snow, author of *Creating Your Own Destiny*, this book would have stayed a "booklet". Patrick has supported and taught me how to put together a professional looking book and how to get connected to the right people to get it published. Besides that, he is one of the most generous and nicest individuals you will ever meet.

Thank you to Michael, Cheryl, Bonnie, Howard and Patrick for sharing your knowledge and experience in business with me! You helped right when I needed help most. I thank you from the bottom of my heart. For your investment of time, energy and kindness, I am truly grateful.

INTRODUCTION

"Who are you?" said the caterpillar …
"I—I hardly know, Sir, just at present," Alice
replied rather shyly, "at least I know who I
was when I got up this morning, but I think
I must have changed several times since then."
—Lewis Carroll

"Nothing heals like the power of a true story. When someone is speaking from the inside of an event, they are speaking from a personal authority that pierces the veil of darkness. On the other side of that veil lies the light of hope, for them and for everyone else."

AND NOTHING IS MORE UPSETTING to your life than unexpected change, yet nothing is as important to your survival as an individual as change. On the front end, our resistance to change is determined by whether we perceive the change as positive or negative and how severe the impact of the change on our lives. On the back-end, it is about how well we are equipped to deal with the change. Our attitude and ultimate acceptance of change is a function of how much resistance we invest in the change as well as the resiliency and coping skills we have developed within our support system. As the Borg in Star Trek would say, "Resistance *(to Change)* is Futile." Change is constant, and we all need to know how to deal with it.

Are you afraid of the unknown? Do you have to both believe and feel that the risks of standing still are greater than those of moving forward? Do you fear not being able to make the transition very well, perhaps fail? We tend to like routines. Familiarity breeds comfort.

I understand these feelings of the unknown and impending failure. For many years following my crash, I dealt with great loss and great change. My biggest fear was that the doctors could be right, that I may never walk, talk understandably or drive. I feared that I would never bring value to anyone in my life, that I would be an anchor and that my support system, the people I loved and cared about, would resent me.

The jewels of experience that are shared in *Achieving NO LIMITS-Embracing Change* prove two life lessons, the power of resiliency (coping skills) and the life-changing influence of choosing to have a positive attitude:

My life experience alone is not sufficient to prove how strong and how resilient the human spirit is. Many others have gone and continue to go through more trying times than I can even imagine. In proving the strength of the human spirit, I mention some of these individuals, but my experiences with despair, loss and rehabilitation are the only ones I can speak to with authority, so my story is where we begin.

I will also prove to you the unbeatable power of an attitude that accepts the things we cannot change. Part of the skills we need in life is about being positive; standing firm, not giving up and making changes in our lives. Positive thinking is real and does work, but it must be balanced with a willingness to accept the inevitable.

Sometimes we need to accept that we cannot have everything we want and that events will not always turn out as we would prefer. We must know that there are some realities we must accept, no matter how painful. I believe that most of our suffering in life comes from fighting what cannot be changed. Learning to focus on what we have instead of what we don't have replaces our immobility with mobility and springboards us back into life. One of the happiest moments you will ever have is when you feel the courage to accept what you cannot change.

Achieving NO LIMITS-Embracing Change follows the plunge from my heights to my depths. Then it explores how I and numerous others have pushed past our comfort zones and faced our fears, finding opportunities for learning and positive growth.

This book shows how our reaction to change is something everyone can control. Once accepted, change can be empowering. We may frequently not have control over the change itself, but we always have control over our reactions to it. Mastering the art of acceptance removes us from the ranks of the victims, those who are controlled by changes, and places us among the victors, those who respond to change by using their power to control their attitudes.

If you want to respond to change with the confidence of a seasoned Sea Captain who looks into a squall and shouts, *"Do your worst for I shall do mine"* then this book is for you; it will give you the steps to build such an attitude. How we habitually respond to our obstacles determines our destiny. The strength of our attitude determines how many obstacles we overcome. That sounds bold, even arrogant, but the people portrayed in this book are proof!

You may have been told that you will only reach a certain level of recovery, yet there are thousands of survivors that surpass the expectations of the healthcare system or other baseline standards. One of the challenges to recovery is that there are no cookie-cutter solutions for rehabilitation. Each individual's injury and healing are different. I believe, in most cases, you can accomplish more than the professionals in the field tell you. All they have to go by are averages, but if you have a stronger support system and you're willing to work harder than the average survivor.

While the challenges many of us face are bigger than anything we imagined, the universal solution is as simple as *A-B-C*. To clearly understand the formula for success that I discovered through my many mentors and role models imagine that we are all born with a book of blank pages.

A is for *Accept the book you have been given.* How thick the book is or whether it is gold-embossed leather bound hardback or a cheaply glued paperback is not up to us, but what the pages will say is up to us.

Achieving NO LIMITS-Embracing Change describes how to live a story people want to read because it fills them with inspiration and hope in their own possibilities. And it shows how following certain steps enabled myself and others live helpful lives and write happy endings. Accepting ourselves and others enables us to be our best and to enjoy positive relationships.

B is for *Believe you can write a happy ending.* Believing we can write happy endings enables us to bounce back from anything. We have choices. In other words, we are in control of our attitudes, which puts us in control of our stories.

C has been the most significant for me. *Caring about others* took the focal point off me and expanded my world of self-inflicted isolation. The real keys to happiness are the intimate connections we have with the people in our lives.

The key to happiness has nothing to do with money, fame, beauty, etc. Happiness is founded on how the people around us treat us. If the people in our lives treat us well, chances are that we are happy. If not, chances are we may not be happy.

My hope is that reading this book inspires you with a W*inners Don't Quit* spirit and attitude. The most important aspect of this spirit is that you will feel and act like a winner because you don't quit **A**ccepting, **B**elieving and **C**aring.

Using all three Winners Don't Quit formulas (**A-B-C**), results in complete acceptance of the way you are and complete acceptance of the way everybody else is; thereby building the connections we need for eternal happiness.

If your dreams do not scare you, they are not big enough. The world will stand aside to let anyone pass who knows where they are going.

There is one thing that we all have in common. That is that at some point in our lives, we will face a life-changing event. It's not a matter of *if,* but rather *when.* I have come to realize that the difference in our success or failure is not the change itself; it's not what happens that will determine our destiny; it's how we react to change.

My hope and desire for you is that your life book includes much happiness! ***Good luck to you!***

CHAPTER 1

What Speed Limit?

*The measure of faith is the degree to which we are willing to
risk telling the truth about what we used to be like,
what happened to us and what we are like now.*
—Pat Mana—"Spiritual Infusion"
(VMI Publications 2009)

DO YOU REMEMBER when you were nineteen-years-old?
What were your hopes, dreams and thoughts of your future? What kind
of values and goals did you have? When I was nineteen, I had an idyllic
life. Everything was going my way. I had everything I wanted or
needed. I loved cars, motorcycles, and one special gal.

My job as a hot-tar roofer earned me enough money to customize
my Camaro and buy a brand new Yamaha 650 Special. To make life
even sweeter, I had a gorgeous girlfriend named Cheryl who wore my
diamond engagement ring.

She loved to ride on the back of my bike, with her arms wrapped
around my waist and her bronze hair flying behind us. I felt good. I was
glad the Christian school I'd been attending expelled me for smoking
weed. Who needed school?

On May 7, 1980, my friend and co-worker Joe Storm and I planned
to meet after work and go to a concert. I stopped by Cheryl's house on
the way to meet him. Time flew by when Cheryl and I got together.
Before I realized it, I was late, "Oh-no!"

I kissed Cheryl one more time then jumped on my bike. The freedom and joy of my life filled my head and heart as I gunned out of the driveway. Wind screamed past my helmet and tore at my leather jacket as I raced down the street. I should have slowed down, but I sped up.

The orange speedometer needle climbed to vertical. I loved the wind in my face. I gave my bike more gas, more gas. I felt free, happy and powerful. I loved the feeling of being in control! Up ahead, teenagers in baseball uniforms stood around the Lake Washington High School baseball diamond.

Wham!

I never saw the pick-up truck that pulled out of a side street right in front of me. Cars packed both sides of the road. People watching the game had tried to park within walking distance. An illegally parked van blocked the view of drivers approaching a stop sign. We've all heard that timing is everything. It sure is! My timing was at exactly the wrong moment. My bike slammed into the truck's front fender, stopping dead and knocking the truck 12 feet sideways. Police estimates said I was going over twice the speed limit.

I shot over the handlebars like I'd been fired from a circus cannon. My head slammed into the front fender of the truck, cracking my helmet and breaking bones in my face. My limp body crumpled to the pavement. Someone called 911.

My heart never quit beating, but because of massive internal hemorrhaging, my blood pressure was too low to read. Paramedics fit me with pressure pants to help squeeze blood from my legs toward my heart and head, buying some time. Smooth and efficient as a Swiss watch, they laid me on a stretcher, loaded me in the medic unit and raced to Harborview Hospital in Seattle.

I was rushed into surgery where doctors removed my spleen and transfused seven and a half pints of blood into me. Considering that the average medium sized individual has ten to eleven pints of blood, I was in serious trouble. No one knew if I would live or die.

The pastor and his wife from my parents' church came to the hospital to be with my parents. A twenty-four-hour prayer vigil began among church members. After two weeks in critical care, I was still comatose, but my vitals had stabilized so they moved me to a private room.

Because of the type of brain injury I'd sustained, a doctor told my parents to start looking for a convalescent home. The hospital's policy indicated that they would have to move me if I didn't wake up within two more weeks. I'm told that when my primary-care physician heard what had been suggested to my parents, he erupted in anger.

I'm not sure if he got mad because he was the one responsible for making decisions about discharge, or because the other doctor's insensitivity made my parents suffer more than they had to. Either way, I whole-heartedly agree with his reported agitation. Why cause more suffering than there already was?

Tears flooded my mom's eyes and ran down her cheeks as I lay in ICU. The doctor told her, "Even if he lives, he'll never be the same." Physically and mentally, she was warned, I'd be a different person. And there'd be behavior changes, maybe drastic changes.

Several years ago, I discovered that my mother had kept a poetic journal of her thoughts during this period. She sent me these lines that I think of as a *Mother's Prayer.*

> **M o t h e r ' s   P r a y e r**
> I'm sorry Lord I thought I was strong.
> I thought I was prepared to face the worst.

> The doctor told me he would never be the same.
> That his intelligence would not reach the same level
> as before the accident.
> That there would be behavior modifications,
> I knew *You* were still in control.
> That out of tragedies, blessings come.
> That no matter what happens,
> *You* can take that thing—that hurt—and
> turn it into something good—turn it into a blessing.

My parents' unwavering faith in God convinced them that blessings would flow from tragedy. Looking back, I realized this provided me courage even though, at the time, I felt nothing but contempt for my situation. Their belief that divine power could rebuild a crushed life gave them strength. Their strength gave me hope. But they were only human. I can't even imagine how they felt when the doctors told them they'd have to start looking for a convalescent home if I didn't wake up soon. My mother's prayer continued:

> The doctor's words kept coming back.
> He won't be the same.
> He may need 24-hour nursing care
> When he leaves here,
> You aren't obligated to take care of him
> The rest of his life.
> But it's too early to tell.
> We don't know how much damage was done to the brain.

Thirty-one days after my crash, I began gradually waking up from my coma. Emerging from a coma is not like waking up from regular sleep. My waking up process was slow and gentle. It was like I was slowly surfacing through different layers of consciousness. I heard voices but couldn't understand what was said. There were blurred images of faces peering down at me and moving away then darkness came again. Consciousness faded in and out. I couldn't tell if I was dreaming or not. Over time, I became aware of my surroundings, staying awake for longer periods of time.

There are amazing stories of coma recovery where brain damaged patients suddenly awaken and start talking to their friends and family. However, these are rare occurrences. In most cases, patients either wake up within a few days or weeks after going into a coma, or remain in a coma or vegetative state for the rest of their lives. I am grateful I woke up after a month and didn't put my parents through more than I had already. I would never have wanted them to be placed in a position to choose a method of care for me the rest of my life or have to decide whether I should live or die.

One result of my crash injuries included paralysis to my larynx, causing my vocal chords to relax and lie together during my month long coma, fusing together. I was asked many questions by the hospital staff, did I know my name; did I know where I was, and so on. Answering these questions blew my mind as my voice was unrecognizable to me and not understandable to others. I sounded like a cross between Sasquatch, a cave man, and a jammed chainsaw. This added more anxiety to my confused, depressed and miserable state of mind.

The "awakening" process is unique for each individual with traumatic brain injury, generally seeing the most improvement within the first six weeks. For a very long time, typically easy things challenged me to choose, understand, remember and use information. Concentrating for more than a few minutes seemed impossible in the beginning. During the first six to eight weeks I started with the emotional and mental age of an infant and slowly progressed. TBI patients can continue to regain cognitive function for many years.

A female therapist would hold up a card with a word printed on it, like "mom" or "home." I would reach out and touch the card and then look at my mother or approval. I was anxious about making too many mistakes.

> That look in his eyes—that longing, forlorn look
> as he struggled to form the word "home"
> the word he had repeated so often the last few days.
> At first he could only searchingly point to
> the letters on the card: H-O-M-E
> Then slowly the sound became intelligent.
> Yes, I want to take you home.
> My heart aches when I see
> your longing eyes, your trusting face.
> Is this why God saved your life?
> Is this what God wants me to do
> with my time and energy—
> to take care of a little boy—
> a trusting little boy who just before his nineteenth birthday
> was a strong, healthy, active, handsome, young man?
> You don't remember your birthday—
> we sang to you as you lay in a coma in ICU.

I was so disoriented I didn't know up from down. I was unable to pay attention for any length of time and was often agitated and frustrated. These feelings were all based in fear. How was I going to live with a disability? How would I do it? For years, this fear kept me locked in a prison of loneliness. Bars of anger and confusion sunk into a foundation of anxiety, keeping meaningful relationships out of reach.

When they raised the head of my bed, my head flopped to the side. Disorientation kept me from knowing up from down. When they would put me in a wheelchair, my head flopped to the side like a big dead fish. For weeks, a strap, called a halo, encircled my head. It was fastened to a vertical bar on the back of my wheelchair. The bar projected a bit higher than my head and kept me upright. My staying upright was more important to Cheryl and my parents than to me since I didn't know when I wasn't upright.

My head injury kept me oblivious to how bad things had actually become. About three months after I came out of my coma, I realized with wrecking-ball abruptness just how much things had changed. Looking back I realize now how my crash affected my entire family. When I crashed, so did they in a different way. They all suffered along with me.

There were so many unanswered questions about the long-term effects of brain injury on my ability to function in the real world. The length of time I was in a coma and the duration of loss of memory (amnesia) following my coma were useful in predicting how well I would recover. I woke up from my coma on the long end range of the general length of time, 2 to 4 weeks, with mine being 31 days.

Do you realize how often in life, when we make a choice to do or not to do something, those choices and actions affect others? Have you ever thought, *"This is my life and I can live it as I choose."* I did. I later learned that my choices do affect others. My brother delayed his plans for college for one year and my parent's lives and dreams were refocused on my rehabilitation, which was long and stressful.

We never know how we affect someone else's life, but we know we do affect others. In the movie, "It's a Wonderful Life" George Bailey didn't know how his life had changed others around him until he was able to SEE it. He had changed others for the better. Without him, his brother had died as a child, his mother was an alcoholic and his uncle was a mess. Remember when he lived, "An angel got his wings." Yes, George had changed others for the positive.

As a professional speaker now, my attitude often is to "Pay it Forward." I may not be able to completely pay back my family that helped direct, guide and steer me along through this tragedy, but I can pay it forward to others by sharing what I have learned.

CHAPTER 2

Never Walk? Never Drive?

Pain is inevitable. Suffering is optional.
—M. Kathleen Casey

HAVE YOU EVER asked for something you ended up not wanting? I not only asked to see Harborview Hospital's chief neurosurgeon, I insisted on it. Finally he visited my room.

He was a big and self-assured man, but as he stood beside my bed, he seemed uncomfortable. Neurosurgeons have outstanding communication skills. They learn to speak clearly and directly in the operating room. This skill comes in handy when explaining the operating procedures and consulting with patients about their health. Many physicians will experience intense emotions of their own when they communicate bad news to a patient.

As I saw him begin to speak, he looked the way I felt when the vet told me my cat was dying from kidney failure and I told him to put her to sleep. While my mind worked slower than before, the adrenaline started pumping and my mind sprinted in slow motion to the worst case scenario. My fight or flight response was preparing to kick in.

My speech was even more garbled from my agitated state of mind. I had to point to letters on an alphabet board to ask him how long he thought it would take before I could walk and drive again. The noises coming from the hospital hallway seemed to fall silent. I held my breath. My beating heart pounded nails into my coffin. Why didn't he answer? His eyes went from looking at the alphabet board to my face as he slowly told me, "You will never be able to walk or drive again."

Most patients want a straightforward honest discussion with their physicians, but also want them to be sensitive enough to provide hope. *Never* seemed like a long time to me.

I panicked. Never walk!? Never drive!? I'm a nineteen-year-old roofer. I have to walk. I have to drive. Talk about being handed a set of limits. Frantically, I threw the bed clothes aside with my one good arm, pushed my paralyzed leg off the bed and tried to stand up.

Why was the room tilted? I reached out to balance myself on the bedside table but missed and fell on my face. The doctor and two nurses put me back in bed like I was some kind of weak, disease-ravished old man. How humiliating. I couldn't leave it there! As soon as they turned around, I climbed back out and fell on my face again. This time they put me back in bed and strapped me in.

Initially, I was in shock and felt numb and did not want to believe it. Slowly I digested the information. As I lay staring at the ceiling, I could see the writing on the wall (which is quite a feat). The belt strapping me to the bed was redundant. Horror swirled in my head and then to my heart and my stomach as I lay frozen to the mattress, wondering what kind of life I'd have. I was too scared to even think about the changes I faced, but an invisible force pulled my mind to where it had never gone before.

The writing on the wall finally stood out clearly: It was like a lighten bolt that come and shook the foundation of the ground around me: instead of hanging out with friends—backpacking, parachuting, snow and water skiing, going to rock concerts and to the beach—I'd be spending my time in rehabilitative therapy—physical therapy, speech therapy, occupational therapy, and psychotherapy.

What kind of life was that? I had always pitied people who had life-changing accidents. Now, understanding the basis of pity, I realize in some way I had felt the person with the misfortune had no recourse or possibility to reverse the situation. Some people who dish out pity even feel inferior to the individual with the bad luck. I could never even imagine it happening to me, but now it had. The impossible had happened: I absolutely did not want to believe it, but I was handed a life-sentence of limitations. I did not want anyone pitying me. I wanted to be "normal" like all my friends. Little did I know then that most of my friends would leave me behind, not so much because they pitied me, but more because I could no longer participate in the things we had once shared.

How would I react to this new life? What did I do to deserve this? What could I have done differently to have altered this miserable outcome? Resolution came slow. The denial stage of grief held me captive.

Life since my motorcycle crash has been unlike anything I have ever known. Having my strong, capable body replaced by a shell of what it had been was like being plucked from a jungle of luscious, colorful fruit and thrown into a desert of heat-blasted sand. Even more dramatic were the changes going on inside my head. My thoughts used to arrive with the speed of Indy cars. Now they plodded along with the sluggishness of mule-drawn wagons on the Oregon Trail. The person I had been was gone. So who was I now?

At Harborview Hospital, nothing mattered but my memory of the great life I'd enjoyed. The doctor's words echoed in my ears: "Never walk or drive again." The dismal future I faced glowed on the wall where the bloodless hand had written its prediction. My life had exploded like a torpedoed battleship. All that remained were bubbles floating on the ocean's surface—the ocean of my life.

All the things that had made me feel like a winner were gone. No high-paying job, no customized Camaro, no beautiful motorcycle. I couldn't even get out of bed! Any possessions I owned were meaningless since I couldn't use them anyway. I did have things of value in my life, but all I focused on was what I had lost.

Initially, the losses made me feel sad, lonely and depressed, even angry at the injustice of my loss for many years to come. I reacted to having a life I loved yanked away and replaced with a life I despised. If I were to put into a nutshell what 30+ years of rehab and hindsight have taught me about great loss, I would say:

Be patient with yourself while you heal through the grieving process.

Recognize that grief needs time and space for the process to unfold, but allow light in the middle of it all. Although there were years of despair that seemed to bleed together like a faded diary dropped in a hot bath, there were days that I experienced joy. I should have embraced those days more often instead of allowing my negative emotions to sabotage my life for so long.

I have become better at getting through loss. As a whole, we all become stronger to better withstand the stress of life by taking these negatives, feeling their impact and growing stronger from them, allowing us to deal with all the feelings that come as a result of loss. It's too bad I didn't know when I was younger the things I know now.

When we lose something precious to us, the grief can be intense. Pain and unanswered questions can haunt us. We will even tell ourselves we'll never get over it, that we'll never laugh or be whole again. Take heart, though there is no way to grieve without pain, there are healthy ways to grieve which allow us to constructively move forward. Don't settle for a life drained of joy. Patiently work through your loss and, slowly but surely, you will get better. Don't sabotage your recovery through impatience or laziness, like I did so many times.

After a serious loss, we sometimes want to do something, anything to dull the pain. Submitting to harmful habit like drug use, alcohol abuse, oversleeping, Internet overuse, or wanton promiscuity threatens our well-being and leaves us vulnerable to addiction and further pain. Only by acknowledging our grief, not sedating it or hiding from it, can we begin to defeat it.

My biggest challenge ahead was learning the ability to overcome my loss and appreciate what I already had instead of wishing I had more. It didn't occur to me until much later in life that some of the very best things in life are intangible; and that I could experience them at any time by opening my heart and mind and letting them in.

At nineteen years, a motorcycle crash forced me to completely reinvent myself physically, mentally, emotionally and socially. Plan A was no longer an option and I didn't have a Plan B. Many folks let these life-changing circumstances define them, but for others, they excel and beat the statistics. Somehow, I was going the beat this and be able to talk, walk and drive again!

CHAPTER 3

Reinventing Myself with Rehab

*"If we look at the world with a love of life,
the world will reveal its beauty to us."*
—Daisaku Ikeda

*"Providence has hidden a charm in difficult undertakings which is
appreciated only by those who dare to grapple with them."*
—Anne-Sophie Swetchine

WHAT ARE THE BEST things about life? If you asked an 8-year old version of me to list all the things I loved best about life, it might have included something like: ice cream, snow days, beach days, more ice cream with cookies and baseball. In fact, I'm sure I could have created an inventory longer than my usual Christmas list, including a ton of things that either tasted, felt or looked good.

However, after my crash, I could see very little about my life that seemed good. I had a supportive family and a girlfriend that stood by me, yet I felt so alone, blanketed in fear. I could not see that no matter how bad things can get, there is always something beautiful to keep us going forward. I did not understand that every moment in life is a chance for a new beginning. These things I slowly learned.

Grandma Moses said it best: Life is what you make it, always has been always will be. Many of us dream of a future that's very different from our present. Getting from where we are, to where we want to be, can be hard because we often chase dreams that are unrealistic, not well planned out or that that align against reinvention.

Without a clear-eyed assessment of our present and our future, and an effective approach to setting, pursuing and achieving goals, we many times end up with a future we really don't want and are unfulfilled, sick, broke or lonely.

Before I could reshape what seemed like a dismal future, I had to be brutally honest about my present. What did I need to accept or change to achieve the new life I wanted? I didn't know if I had it in me, but I had to try. I wanted my life back and I knew it would be a daunting journey. I wanted to feel like a winner again, so I continued to envision a setting in which my future self would be happier.

In other words, life may be tough at times, but we can choose to be winners or losers. Losers choose to see calamities and limitations everywhere they look. Winners choose to see challenges and opportunities.

Rehabilitation has been a series of challenges, allowing me to reinvent myself. My first goals after waking from my coma sound simpler than they actually were—things like learning to sit in a wheelchair without my head flopping to the side due to lack of orientation and decreased neck strength from the left side paralysis and pulling me to the floor. Learning to dress myself, pull on my socks and tie my shoes with my one good hand. Learning to hold my water till I reached the bathroom was a big deal at the time. Goals like these filled my days at the beginning of my rehabilitation.

I also could not control the drooling from my mouth. Because of my impaired neuromuscular control where the voluntary oral motor activity stopped functioning (throat/mouth), an overflow of saliva drooled from the left side of my mouth. Additionally, I had a hard time swallowing, which didn't help. I would often choke on my saliva. That always got me a lot of attention. It was as if I could see myself from outside of myself, watching everyone hover around me. At the time, I knew things had to change, but I wondered if they ever would.

At first glance, the physical goals facing me seemed tough. But a tougher, more elusive goal was keeping my spirits up. How can you be happy when you have gone from having a life every eighteen-year-old wants to having a life no nineteen-year-old wants?

Rehabilitation seemed impossible at first, but as they say, "Necessity is the mother of invention." Over time, I discovered ways to build and maintain a positive spirit by accomplishing small goals and believing I could do more. When my spirits were high, I felt as if I could do anything. But if my spirits were down, even routine obstacles seem insurmountable. I'd become restless, irritable and discontent.

My head injury ruptured my brain stem, which serves as a type of control tower that sends messages to individual muscles. The muscles on my left side were intact, but they wouldn't move because they weren't receiving any messages from the control tower. And, even worse, my hypothalamus gland ruptured. The hypothalamus helps regulate and stabilize emotions.

Sun streamed through the open window and fresh air filled the hospital's Physical Therapy Room as I lay on my back on the PT mat and Cynthia, my therapist, knelt beside me, holding my elbow.

"Al," she said, "let me see you straighten your arm." I didn't expect it to budge. It hadn't moved last time or the time before that, but I gave it a shot. My mouth popped open as my arm straightened and my hand rose toward the ceiling. I was shocked! Part of my triceps had heard the command to move.

I wish Cynthia had been able to work her magic on the rest of my muscles or on my ruptured hypothalamus. Interacting normally with people is tough when you erupt like a volcano without warning. As a matter of fact, the Volcano Mount St. Helens in Washington State erupted on May 18, 1980, eleven days after my crash, sending out a plume of ashes that were still visible when I came out of my coma. Was this a coincidence? Some folks probably think so.

One of my first limitations was not being able to walk. My goal became to walk using a specially made walker with one handle in the middle. Once I learned to use the walker to totter across the physical therapy room, my next goal was to hobble down the hall to the office where I took speech therapy.

One day, with me gripping the walker and my fiancée gripping the belt around my waist, my physical therapist walked behind us pushing my wheelchair giving instructions like, "Stand straighter. Take the same size steps with both feet. Slow down. Stop kissing your girlfriend."

Even with me leaning on the walker, it still took a couple months of trying before I could cover the thirty yards from the PT room to the speech therapy office. I can still remember how proud I felt the first time I made it. I remembered how, in the not-too-distant past, I carried a full backpack twenty-five miles over hilly terrain and now I was struggling to hobble down a short hallway. What was wrong with me? I felt OK. Why wouldn't my muscles do what I told them? I couldn't have made it without using that walker and having someone holding my safety belt.

The only thing I hated more than that walker was the fact that I couldn't walk without it. Once, I hurled it across the empty PT room in frustration. It crashed into the wall and clattered to the floor. Taking two months to build up to hobbling all the way down the hall didn't seem like much of an accomplishment.

But looking back on it now, a few decades later, those two months seem incredible. I spent the first year after I was out of the hospital making the shift from a quad-cane to a one-point cane. I spent the next sixteen years trying to appear stable while I limped along with no cane at all. Two months were nothing. It took a while, but today I admit that if I don't have to carry something in my good hand, I look and feel more stable when I use a cane.

Because my vocal chords fused together during the coma, my voice sounded like a jammed chainsaw. Talk about embarrassing. I had to repeat myself again and again. I'd get super mad. People thought I was angry with them when I was just mad at my situation. Back in the hospital, a speech therapist helped my enunciation by having me repeat short phrases over and over, emphasizing a different word each time. Her favorite phrase to have me repeat was:

***WINNERS** Don't Quit! Winners **DON'T** Quit!! Winners Don't **QUIT**!!!*

I took physical and speech therapy for seven years. The therapists I saw after getting out of the hospital had me recite words and phrases into a tape recorder. Not only did the tape help me adjust the way I sounded, analyzing my speech helped me notice that I was actually getting better. Setting goals and tracking my progress at overcoming limits raised my spirits.

While in the hospital, my speech impairment was so bad that when hospital visitors heard my barking, they thought they were in the Seattle Aquarium. A few other patients at the time had similar speech impairments.

Those days aren't the clearest in my memory, so some of the details of actual events are a bit fuzzy. The following event is one example that either happened one night or I dreamed that four of us speech impaired wheelchair riders were sitting in our chairs by the nurse's desk, impatiently waiting for our afternoon snacks.

A young woman stepped off the elevator and heard us barking away. She got excited and pulled her husband toward us. "Come on, Honey, let's feed the seals." One reason I happen to remember this is because she happened to have a purse full of freshly caught fish.

She pulled them out one by one and started tossing them to us. Our wheelchairs crashed together as we raced around with our mouths wide open. A few fish hit the floor, but we caught most of them. We didn't complain that our snacks were late. Why would we?

At age eighteen, I saw myself as a confident winner. At nineteen, I saw myself as a complete loser. And because I saw myself as a loser, I was a loser. Over the years, I've realized that just because everything was going my way when I was eighteen didn't mean I was a winner. And just because nothing seemed to be going my way when I was nineteen didn't mean I was a loser.

Life's circumstances don't determine a person's value. How we choose to see life's circumstances and how we respond to those circumstances is what makes us winners or losers. Losers see calamities in every challenge. Winners see challenges in every calamity. Whether I choose to see challenges or calamities is entirely up to me.

Choices are the most powerful freedom we have. Choices will either make us or break us. One choice at a time, we're either building our castle or our coffin. A scary thing about choices is that it takes a whole series of good choices to improve your life, but only one bad choice can destroy your life. It did mine.

Every day we have the opportunity to reinvent ourselves into a more positive version of ourselves. We are always in motion, but we decide every day, are we going forward or backward? It is our choice. Major life changes are never easy, but when we learn to focus on what our future could be, supported by goals, we can achieve much more than many people would ever think. I know I have surprised a lot of folks. I've even surprised myself.

CHAPTER 4

Cherishing a Lost Romance

Love can sweep you off your feet and carry you along in a way you've
never known before. But the ride always ends,
and you end up feeling lonely and bitter. Wait.
It's not love I'm describing. I'm thinking of a monorail.
—Jack Handey
No man or woman really knows what perfect love is until they have been
married a quarter of a century.
—Mark Twain's *Notebook*

"SWEETIE I LOVE YOU," Cheryl said. Thick lashes surrounded her big brown eyes. Cheryl's eyes took away my fears. Her words made me feel like I could do anything. But whenever she'd leave, and we were no longer physically together, what worried me was that I wasn't the same person she agreed to marry before my crash.

I loved her so much it hurt, but my feelings for her were like an iron necklace—a necklace of fear. She was a beautiful woman who could have her pick of guys. Why would she want to marry a cripple? She seemed fine with it right then, but how long would it last? There are plenty of guys who have it together so much better than I do, who would jump at the chance to be with her.

Everyone remembers their first love. I'd had girlfriends and crushes before Cheryl but nothing could compare to my feelings for

Cheryl. My family had moved from Michigan to Washington State when I was in 7th grade. Cheryl was in 9th grade at the time.

I was immediately drawn to her the first time I set my eyes on her. I still remember watching her walk down the hall. She had a perfect figure and her hair was a cross between the color of a shiny new penny and golden blonde. Her face was worthy of Michelangelo's best effort. She was the most amazing female I had ever encountered.

We knew of each other, and like other red-blooded guys, I dreamed of going out with her, but our knowledge of each other's existence stayed at the impersonal level of saying hi when we happened to see each other around school. We went to the same school for one more year after that first year, then she left and I forgot about her. At least I forgot about her as much as it's possible to forget about the most beautiful woman you can imagine.

After getting kicked out of my last year of high school for smoking pot, I took a job as a hot tar roofer. This dirty and potentially dangerous job paid well. After nearly two years of solid work, my rewards included a customized Camaro and a beautiful Yamaha 650 Special. And I had money to spare.

One day, a new roofer got hired and put on my crew. "You ever done any roofing?" I asked.

Glen smiled and shook his head. "Figured I'd try it for a while; my wife Shelly told me Lee was hiring." My ears pricked up. *Cheryl has a sister named Shelly.* After a few pertinent questions, I learned that not only was Glen Cheryl's brother in-law, Cheryl was staying with a family I knew and she was currently single!

After my third date with Cheryl, my Camaro rumbled as I pulled into the dead-end side street that ran along her driveway. I killed the engine and turned to look at her. She looked back at me with her big brown eyes. I often recall the words of singer-songwriter, musician and guitarist, Bob Marley's song 'Brown Eyed Girl.'

I've been watching you, a-la-la-la-la-long a-la-la-la-la-long-long-lee-long-long-long; Come on –a-la-la-la-la-long a-la-la-la-la-long-long-lee-long-long-long; Standing across the room I saw you smile; Said I wanna talk to you for a little while; But before I make my move, my emotions start running wild, my tongue gets tied, and that's no lie; I'm looking in your eyes; I'm looking in your big brown eyes.

She stretched her arms out in front of her and set her perfectly manicured hand in plain view. It seemed so tantalizingly close and yet so far away. I had butterflies in my stomach. What if I tried to take her hand and she didn't want me to be so forward? What if I made her feel uncomfortable and scared her away? What if she said *Let-go!*? I imagined her getting out of the car and never wanting to see me again. Obviously, I had very little experience and I looked back into her eyes and nearly got lost.

Finally, I said, "Your hands are beautiful!"

"Thanks," she quietly said.

I took her hand in mine. "These are really nice," I said admiring her well-manicured nails. She didn't resist and before I knew it, our fingers were entwined. We sat holding hands and making small talk for who knows how long. Time flew or stood still. All I knew is I was in heaven. Shadows grew longer as the sun started falling behind the Seattle skyline.

"I better get inside," she finally said.

"OK, I said. "Thanks for going out with me today."

She looked at me, "Of course. It was fun." We both leaned forward and like we were following the script of my dream, we both closed our eyes and began slowly kissing. It was one of the most memorable moments of my life.

The following weeks and months were filled with going out for meals, exploring the Ocean Shores community and when it started to snow, four of us, my friend Joe and Cheryl's and my friend Michelle from our school days went up skiing.

On a sunny day in April, about one month before my motorcycle crash, Cheryl and I were returning from flying our big orange kite at Marymoor Park. I circled the cul-de-sac I lived in. Before backing into my driveway, I looked at Cheryl.

"I want to marry you," I said with a heart that felt euphoric.

"I want to marry you, too," she said. Her big doe-like brown eyes sparkled with warmth and acceptance.

When I think back to that moment, I remember a few lyrics from a song from Jeff Healy that was actually released in 1988 called 'Angel Eyes.'

Girl, you're lookin' fine tonight; And every guy has got you in his sights. What you're doin' with a clown like me? It's got to be one of life's little mysteries. So tonight I'll ask the stars above, how did I ever win your love, what did I do, what did I say, to turn your angel eyes my way?

"Al," Cheryl said again, nudging my arm to get my attention. I forced my mind back to the current moment where we sat in the hospital and looked at her.

"What are you thinking about?" she asked.

"I shrugged. "Nothing, I wonder what's taking my therapist so long."

"Yeah, I wonder too." Cheryl looked down the hall toward the physical therapy room, and I plunged back into my thoughts. What hurt was not my love for Cheryl, my love for her felt great. What hurt was my fear of losing her.

At 19, my understanding of women was even more limited than it is now. In retrospect, I can see how my belief was who *I* was physically and who *she* was physically was the most important part of our relationship. By focusing on the physical aspects of which we were, to the exclusion of the other parts, I didn't give myself credit for who I was or who I could evolve into. And I didn't see who Cheryl really was or who she could become.

Cheryl was the last vestige of the life I'd loved. I clung to her as if she was a life preserver and I was a sea captain who'd been knocked off the deck of his battleship. Everywhere I looked, seemingly insurmountable obstacles—like relearning to talk, walk, drive, dress and feed myself—took on the shape of hungry sharks. Sharks that kept circling me like keeping me from becoming the man a beautiful young woman wants and deserves was their only goal.

Articles on first loves in *Psychology Today* validate the trouble I've had forgetting the feelings I had for Cheryl. *Psychology Today* says: "Early romantic experiences can leave a lasting imprint on who we are—and who we fall for."

"I love you, too, Babe," I said. Cheryl sat in a chair facing my wheelchair and I leaned forward far enough to kiss her soft lips. After I came out of my coma, and once I could understand what he was talking about, my psychologist warned Cheryl and I that I wasn't emotionally capable of understanding and dealing with the feelings that accompany a physical relationship. Did we listen? No. Am I sorry we didn't? Absolutely!

That was one of the best pieces of advice I ever ignored. What we desperately needed at that moment was a leader to whom we would have both listened. If one of us had been willing to firmly insist that we heed the advice of those who had experience, things could have turned out far better. In retrospect, I see how I missed a golden opportunity to not only provide Cheryl with the comfort she needed, but possibly to save a relationship headed for the rocky coast surrounding the ocean of life.

Intellectually, I was slower than before, but I could still understand the instructions we were given. My problem was that physically I was a young man, but emotionally I was a toddler. Our intellect, physical desires, and emotional maturity are completely separate. Even an intellectual or physical giant can be as emotionally immature as a kid. Look around, well publicized court cases that are steadily becoming less and less isolated prove that even police officers and judges, pillars of our communities, can make selfish and destructive decisions because of emotional immaturity and an entitlement attitude.

I will never forget our *first time*. Cheryl and I were in my room on Harborview Hospital's rehab floor. I'd finished my various therapies for the day and we were just hanging out.

"Come on, Cheryl. We're gonna do it all the time after we get married. What difference does it make if we begin a little early?" I was probably the first guy in the history of the world to use a variant of that line. Not.

Our love might have been totally genuine and lasted a lifetime, but because we never had any long, heart-to-heart talks about what we both wanted out of our relationship, we never even found out if we wanted the same things. Maybe we did, but maybe we didn't. Of course at our age, our dreams and goals were still taking shape anyway.

It's not that we were opposed to sharing our dreams and goals. I distinctly remember one conversation in which we almost had a revealing conversation about our dreams and goals, but that conversation ended with us feeling so close and comfortable that we started kissing and completely forgot about what we had been talking about.

To be realistic about my love for Cheryl, I have to acknowledge that we were both under the influence of some powerful hormones. Remember the saying is not "staying balanced in love"; it is "falling", "losing yourself to love." We were both young and lost ourselves in each other; and we didn't take the advice provided by a professional phycologist.

Cheryl wanted to give me the comfort I craved, which wasn't the comfort I needed. What I needed, what we both needed, was the willingness and the maturity to delay gratification and heed the advice of the well intentioned rehab psychologist. However, at this point, my accident had been too recent to add any maturity to either of us. I completely missed my opportunity to lead us into a place that would have ultimately been the softer and easier way.

And what about what Cheryl needed or wanted? When I look back, I often thought about how her closeness and comfort would make me feel. Instead I should have been thinking about how I could make her happy. Loving someone is when their happiness means more than your own. Unfortunately, I got lost in the eutrophic feeling of "falling in love."

Why did I miss the opportunity to explore what made her happy? Was it because I was reckless, irresponsible and rebellious? That's part of it. Part of it is also that we were both trying to fill the hole my crash punched in our lives and that we were not mature enough to handle without outside help.

The real problem was that neither Cheryl nor I were humble enough to be teachable. We both thought we knew enough to ignore the advice of the psychologist. Not only did I pass up the opportunity to establish myself as a responsible leader in the relationship, I passed up the opportunity to strengthen our crash weakened relationship.

Albert Einstein wrote: *"How on earth are you ever going to explain in terms of chemistry and physics so important a biological phenomenon as first love?"* In a similar way as a sexually abused kid, the results of our irresponsible behavior took me years of counseling and uncomfortable effort to eradicate.

The process cost me time, money, embarrassment, broken relationships, and tons of heartache. I paid a price for ignoring the psychologist's advice. I could not walk away from what had happened. My mind was as impressionable as a child's in the same way that a child's earliest experiences influence what the adult considers normal later in life. My fiancée's and my behavior cut psychological tracks in my thinking that took nearly two decades of on again, off again counseling to erase.

More than a few psychologists told me that I was having problems with relationships because I was unconsciously using the same behaviors that had been successful with Cheryl with every new girl I met. I was embarrassed at my behavior and intimidated by the enormity of its psychological causes. I couldn't even think of including this aspect of my rehabilitation in my talks to students in school assemblies, or in this book, or even in my stand-up comedy routine until counseling helped me eliminate the problem and strengthen my crumbling self-esteem.

Today, I earn my living sharing what a traumatic brain injury and decades of rehabilitation have taught me. During certain parts of my presentations, it would now be unthinkable to not mention the havoc that having sex before I was psychologically and emotionally ready cost me. It destroyed my social life for almost twenty years!

After Cheryl left me, I wanted a duplicate of Cheryl and the comforts she provided. And because of my brain damage, it took a long time for me to rebuild new tracks in my mind and relearn the skills on how to have healthy adult relationships.

For nearly two decades, I was in and out of counseling sessions to help me create and maintain healthy relationships. Looking back over the nearly 35 years since my crash, I can happily say that I am blessed with meaningful relationships and with the ability to maintain those relationships. Time takes time. Learning new skills takes humility and willingness.

I've set and reached a ton of goals since my injury, but rediscovering that women can be colleagues and friends is one of my most valuable and enjoyable rehabilitative victories. As I look back on my relationship with Cheryl from the comfort of a rebuilt life, I'm sure it was a combination of things that tore us apart.

More than anything, it was the change in my attitude that led to our separation. The combination of losing everything I had, plus losing my ability to get any of it back, changed me from a happy, confident young man to a self-absorbed, angry, bitter person wrapped in self-pity. Wow, that must have been attractive, just what every girl dreams of—Not!

Our attitude is one of the most powerful things we have. Attitude is a choice. The attitude we choose can either make us or break us; it will either build our castle or our coffin.

Painful as it was, my fiancée's leaving me was apparently typical for couples in the situation we were in. Articles, therapists and doctors tell me that broken relationships happen in the vast majority of cases involving life-altering injuries. I felt terrible that Cheryl left, but I also cherish the memories of the good times we shared before she was gone. I could have saved myself decades of pain and a score of friendships if only we'd listened and waited until we were both ready.

The truth is that neither of us could leave it totally behind us. Cheryl's pain was as real as mine. She hung in there with me after the crash for about a year. I can't imagine how hard that must have been on her. She filled up her life helping me through my first year of disability and rehabilitation. She was my coach in many ways. I knew I had to perform to hang on to her so I pushed myself as much as I could. However, I was so needy and clingy and so desperate, always afraid of losing her. I remember her trying her best to be what I needed, but I always needed more, more, more. I'm surprised she lasted a year, many would have walked away much quicker.

I heard through the grapevine that this beautiful girl who became a registered nurse and then got her master's degree in nutrition, both after my crash, never found a solid relationship. Nearly twenty years after my crash, I got home to find a couple phone messages from her on my answering machine. This shook me up, especially when a short time later, I received an invitation to her funeral. She had apparently committed suicide. Sweet, sweet, dear Cheryl, were you calling for help? Was I too caught up in something that I don't even remember to hear your cry? I had lost Cheryl once again.

Suicide is *not* a pointless or random act. To people who think about ending their own lives, suicide represents an answer to an otherwise insoluble problem or a way out of some unbearable dilemma. It is a choice that is somehow preferable to another set of dreaded circumstances, emotional distress, or disability, which the person fears more than death. Suicide offers oblivion, an escape. *I had been there more than once.*

Phycology Today says that often, people with high standards and expectations are especially vulnerable to ideas of suicide when progress toward these goals is suddenly frustrated. People who attribute failure or disappointment to their own shortcomings may come to view themselves as worthless, incompetent or unlovable.

I wish I had answered the phone and had talked to her. Maybe I could have redirected her plans. *Phycology Today* also says that one of the most harmful myths about suicide is the notion that people who really want to kill themselves don't talk about it. Most people who commit suicide have told other people about their plans. And most people are not trained to respond adequately to these calls for help. It is estimated that in at least 80 percent of completed suicides, the people provide verbal or behavioral clues that indicate clearly their lethal intentions.

During the crisis that precipitates suicidal thoughts, people generally employ the same response patterns that they have used throughout their lives. For example, people who have refused to ask for help in the past are likely to persist in that pattern, increasing their sense of isolation.

Cheryl wasn't the type of person to ask for help, at least when I knew her. She was the giver. If only I had been home when she called, perhaps she would still be alive. Perhaps that's preposterous of me to assume that I could have made a difference, but my love her had been genuine, and I would have tried to help.

Falling in love is like a pretty powerful drug. When we feel it, we ***really*** feel it. It can suspend time, making the whole world seem still except for the two individuals. It feeds us more than any nourishment; we feel full in the presence of love.

But there's a vast difference between love and *true* love. True love knows no depth. It's an endless tunnel that sweeps you up in the whirlwind and we're never quite free from it. It stays with you. And you hope this person will too. True love isn't ordinary. It doesn't come around often and that's how you'll know it's genuine.

Cheryl was my first love and it felt like *true* love as I still love her today. Whether or not it would have lasted over time had I not had my crash, I will never really know. All I do know is that our first romance, first love, is something so special to all of us, both emotionally and physically, that it touches our lives and enriches them forever.

CHAPTER 5

Re-Focusing With a Little Help

We don't like their sound, and guitar music is on the way out.
—Decca Recording Company, rejecting the Beatles, 1962

HAVE YOU EVER BEEN to a rock concert? My arm hung over Cheryl's shoulders as we made our way among the thousands of people waiting to see Bruce Springsteen in concert. The Boss! I'd seen him before my accident and I was psyched about seeing him again. Concerts had been a passion of mine ever since I saw my first Aerosmith show three or four years before.

Eric Clapton, The Who, the Grateful Dead, the Doobie Brothers, Bad Company, Aerosmith and many others I've seen were all good. But, in my opinion, back in the late '70s and very early '80s, Bruce Springsteen was the Boss.

Hobbling along with Cheryl's help, most people probably thought I was too drunk to walk on my own. I know the police officers at the door to the coliseum thought I was. At least they thought I was until they tried to give me the typical search and Cheryl let them know right then what was up. They didn't search me. They didn't even search her, or my friend Joe Storm, who I had worked with as a roofer and who was walking with us into the concert. It always amazes me how much instant respect a good looking, fiery-eyed woman can get from total strangers, especially when she's got the power of right on her side.

Joe and I had gone to a ton of concerts together before my accident. The Boss was one of a handful of bands you have to see at least twice. He put on a longer, harder rocking show than anyone I'd ever seen. Springsteen's show sold out, so we hadn't been able to get three seats together.

We had two seats on the floor and one in the third row of the stands. Once inside, we made our way to the two seats on the floor. Joe, who had gotten the tickets, being his typical cool self, said to Cheryl, "You sit down here with Al. I'll sit in this other seat for a while; then we'll switch for a while." She nodded, "Okay." Joe patted me on the back and disappeared.

The concert crowd seemed pretty calm, but with thousands of people talking, the noise was still pretty loud. Then the lights went out. Everything got quiet. Cheryl and I clung to each other. Suddenly the stage exploded with multi-colored lights and electric sound. The crowd went crazy as a hit song engulfed us.

Cheryl and I looked at each other and started kissing. What could be better than this? Our kiss lasted three or four songs. Suddenly Joe reappeared. He was a great friend, and if it wasn't for him we wouldn't have even been there, but I didn't think about anything except what I wanted. And at the moment I wanted to keep kissing Cheryl.

Have you ever felt that your own needs or wants were more important than anyone else's? One way my brain injury affected me, as traumatic brain injuries tend to do, was to almost force me to focus on my own needs and wants. This limited my ability to care about others. I didn't purposely put other people's interests beneath mine; it's just that my own interests seemed so significant that it didn't even occur to me that other people have needs, too.

I completely forgot that Joe had purchased the tickets for all of us and that he was a good friend. I forgot everything but my immediate wants. All I knew was that I had been enjoying kissing Cheryl and I wanted her to stay.

It's been over 30 years, but I can still remember how I sat there without really listening to the music. I just sat there and pouted because Cheryl was gone. I still recall this incident because those same selfish concerns for my own needs at that time has cost me a number of friendships over the years. Friendships are like bank accounts. You can't take more out than you put in.

As time passed from my traumatic brain injury (TBI) until now, I gradually became aware of other people's needs. As this awareness grew, I had to consciously not criticize myself too severely for my earlier selfish behavior. Self-criticism helps no one, and it hurts the criticizer.

Doing stand-up comedy in nightclubs and then progressing to delivering motivational talks for students in schools, elementary through university levels, helped me get my life going in a positive direction. The responsibility of speaking before audiences really helped improve my attitude and my ability to get along with people. With an improved attitude, life became a little smoother. And with a smoother life came an even better attitude. Right now my attitude is so good I can barely recognize myself.

How do you treat folks with physical or mental impairments? In my experience, people generally react to people with a TBI in one of three ways. Those who have been around long enough to develop some compassion, tend to give people with a TBI the benefit of the doubt, which is welcome if it's done in a non-patronizing way. Other people are so ignorant that they either assume the physically apparent results of a TBI, like paralysis or speech impairment, are the only real consequences. And others assume that physical impairment means that the impaired person is as dumb as a post.

Even though half my body was paralyzed and the TBI had interfered with my thinking and emotional processes, that didn't mean I was stupid. It meant that my speed of thought was dramatically reduced and in stressful or hurried situations, the conclusions I reached could be way off the mark.

The wider the range of experiences a person has had, the larger that person's capacity is for dealing with people like me who may do or say things that are unexpected or inappropriate. My own ability to deal with folks who are not "normal" has grown drastically as a result of my having lived for nearly 34 years now with a TBI. Because educating the entire public, many of whom refuse to be enlightened, is unrealistic, people with a TBI must either adapt or move to a TBI commune.

With his stereo blasting so loudly I could hear him coming down the block, my friend Eric rolled up in his van and parked in my driveway. The Eric Clapton concert didn't begin for another couple hours, so we had plenty of time.

I came out on the porch as Eric rolled down his window and shouted, "Let's go, Dude. It'll take an hour to get down there, plus we've still gotta get some beer." Gripping my cane, I hobbled out to his van. Joe had moved back to New Jersey, and I'd begun going to concerts with a new friend named Eric Robson. A few years older than I am, he's been a guitarist in rock bands for years before becoming lead guitarist with "Solar Wind," a popular jazz band.

My friendship with Eric has lasted for more than 3 decades because he understands people's differences. He knows that people don't always fit our expectations. Learning to accept people, without expecting them to be any certain way, has been one of the most valuable lessons I've learned from Eric and from my own experiences with TBI folks and people in general.

CHAPTER 6

Accepting Circumstances

There is luxury in self-reproach. When we blame ourselves,
we feel that no one else has a right to blame us.
It is the confession, not the priest that gives us absolution.
—Oscar Wilde

OUR VERY FIRST PROBLEM IS TO ACCEPT our present circumstances as they are, ourselves as we are, and the people about us as they are. This is attitude to adopt a realistic humility without which no genuine advance can even begin. Again and again, we will need to return to that unflattering point of departure. This is an exercise in acceptance that we can profitably practice every day of our lives.

"What was it like for you?" Cindy asked as she turned her wheelchair toward me. Because I'm fairly outgoing and because I like to hear other perspectives, I'll frequently talk with people in wheelchairs or those who look like they've had a rough time. When I saw Cindy's wheelchair at a table outside a coffee café, I went over and started talking with her.

"Wow," I said, after hearing Cindy's description of what she saw while she was in her coma. Apparently she had witnessed a dark tunnel and a bright light.

"I knew the light was total love," she said. "Tell me what your coma was like."

I shrugged. I was tempted to make up some kind of fantastic story about bright lights, dark tunnels, and angels, but it seemed kind of silly. Many people have asked if I have any memory of the time I was in a coma. They go on to describe different out-of-body, near death experiences they either had or heard of someone else having while comatose.

If it is possible to have such an experience, I wish I'd had one. That way I would be more inclined to believe folks who say they did. But I didn't, so I don't. OK, so I'm a cynic. Sue me.

One year after my accident, Cheryl left me. With my cane lying on the floor beside the recliner, I slouched into the overstuffed chair staring at the TV, but I saw nothing. What would happen to me? Would I ever get married? Would I ever have another girlfriend as pretty as Cheryl? Would I ever have another good job? Would I ever have any of the things I'd once had or do any of the things I took for granted? I'd been on top of the world, now I was in the pit of hell. My pet terrier sat on the floor beside me. I patted his head. Why couldn't I have been a dog?

Cheryl and I had started attending church a few weeks before my accident. I thought I was making God happy, but apparently not. Who is God? Who knows what God wants?

God is different to different people. But no matter whether a person thinks God is a light bulb or a doorknob or the Creator, I think times of trouble are times when most people turn to their idea of God and ask for help. But, because my accident coincided with when I started going to church, I was torn. Half of me wanted to ask for help, but the other half of me remembered what had happened last time I had showed an interest in spiritual things.

Thick gray clouds and cool autumn air made this a typical October Sunday. I was hobbling around the block. Many times in the first ten years of recovery, I asked God "Why did *You* let this happen? And if it was *You* who let it happen, why did You have to wake me up from my coma? And if it was You who woke me up, why didn't *You* wake me up all the way up? Why did *You* have to leave half my body paralyzed?"

I kept hobbling along with my cane held off the ground. I staggered to a stop, planted my cane on the ground to keep my balance then looked up at the sky.

"Answer me! Why did *You* do it? Health, possessions, relationships, I had everything I wanted. Then I went back to church and now I've got nothing. Why?"

In disgust, I spit on the sidewalk. Who am I talking to? Next I'll be seeing bright lights and dark tunnels. "If You're up there, or out there, You should've let me die!"

Because I had based my happiness on my circumstances, until I accepted my new circumstances, I felt no joy. When I say "accept my circumstances," I'm not saying that I quit doing everything I could to get back as many of my physical capabilities as possible—not at all.

Accepting what had happened to me didn't give me an excuse to not do my best to become everything I could. Just the opposite! When I finally accepted what had happened to me, I quit being angry over what happened and I quit being full of self-pity. I began seeing my new limitations as challenges that could be either overcome or dealt with.

Accepting myself as a person with a disability means accepting my limitations and it also means accepting responsibility for making the most of the abilities I still have. For example, I still have a sense of humor and I still love to write. Although I can no longer be productive at a job requiring physical strength and dexterity or quick decision making, there are certain things I can still do.

For me, accepting my disability includes changing my outlook and my occupation and becoming productive in a new way. Until I finally accepted myself as a person with different strengths from the ones I had before, my attitude made me so hard to deal with people frequently chose not to be around me.

For years I thought other people's perception of my disability was my biggest handicap, but now I can see that my negative attitude was the bigger handicap. In the long run, and sometimes even in the short run, my attitude is more important than my physical attributes. My attitude determines people's perception of my disability.

Partly because of fear that they will make a bad situation even worse and partially because they just don't care to deal with a potentially awkward situation, folks tend to shy away from people with disabilities. And, in my experience, if the person with a disability also has a negative attitude, people don't just shy away, they run away.

Of course they run away. We all have stuff we'd rather not deal with. The last thing any sane person wants is to spend time with someone who wastes time brooding about his troubles, which is why I used spend a lot of time alone. I was hungry for companionship, but I was a miserable companion.

I was a living paradox. Since I wanted friends, I tried to pull people into my life. My friendly approach invited them in, but my negative attitude pushed them back out.

Before acceptance came, I had it in my head that if I just tried hard enough, I'd be able to make my life just as it was before. With that in mind, I lunged after my goals of talking, walking, and driving like a wild gorilla might lunge after a run-away banana cart. Instead of having the peace that eventually came with acceptance, I had a constant feeling of alienation and desperation.

I was desperate to recapture the life I had, but my negative attitude alienated potential friends. Accepting my situation freed me from the ball-and-chain negative attitude I had been dragging around. And once the chain broke, I was free to focus on goals that would make the most out of what I had left.

My primary goals of talking, walking, and driving a car excited my imagination. But in the beginning, they were too far out of reach to waste time focusing on. Luckily, I had a whole string of smaller goals to worry about, like not drooling out of the paralyzed side of my mouth, tying my shoe-laces with one hand, and controlling my bladder till I reached the bathroom so I could quit wearing a catheter.

These goals sound minor, but when you wet yourself in someone else's new car, like I did, it would have been nice to be able to either walk away before they returned or at least do some quick explaining, but all I could do was to sit there drooling.

In memory of events like the one I just mentioned, not needing to wear a catheter was a fairly happy goal to reach. Aiming for and reaching clearly defined goals was a key part of my early rehab. Goal reaching contributed to raising my self-esteem. The way I feel about myself has everything to do with how I feel about people and with what I try to accomplish.

One of my earliest goals was to go to college and become an accountant. How I came up with the idea of being an accountant is a mystery to me. It's a good choice for someone with a healthy brain who also enjoys tedious, repetitive work. Someone like me taking accounting was like trying to teach a baboon to play chess. Not only did it take me an absurdly long time to understand new concepts, I couldn't concentrate for more than a few minutes at a time.

But I had one vital ingredient. I had tenacity. And I had all the time in the world. To make a long story shorter, I'll just tell you I never did manage to cram enough accounting principles into my brain to get a degree in it. But, since I had started college and since I had nothing else to do, I was determined to finish some kind of degree. Luckily, I was going to a two-year college.

I began college a year and a half after my crash. Although academics were my apparent reason for going, my real focus was learning to do the things I needed to do without being angry and bitter, or ashamed of the new me.

The day before the first day of class, I went to speak with the teacher. She called me into her office. "You wanted to see me?"

"Yes."

Suddenly I felt very stupid. Maybe this wasn't such a great idea. But I was afraid what would happen if I didn't do it. She was looking at me. I cleared my throat.

"Ms. (I forget her name), my speech impairment makes people think I'm retarded. I was wondering if, on the first day of class, it'd be OK if I told everybody why I talk the way I do."

She looked about my mom's age. She might have had kids about my age. Her expression said she understood what I was feeling.

"You don't need to," she said. "But if it's something you want to do, you can."

My embarrassment over my speech impairment was pretty severe but it never kept me from speaking my mind. College students seemed to be less preoccupied with my speech impairment than most people in the general public, and after that first class, I quit feeling a need to explain myself.

In fact, being treated well by college students was the first in a series of experiences that gave me confidence to expect the same from other people, and this confidence took away a lot of the intimidation I felt around groups of noisy, laughing, talking people. Trying to interact with a lot of people at once remained frustrating and difficult for quite a while, but it eventually became easier and easier to do it with an ever-increasing level of comfort.

In order to enjoy mingling in crowds, I had to change my expectations. The same rules for one-to-one courtesy and thoughtfulness apply, but since I don't speak or think as quickly and clearly as I used to, I had to learn to hold my tongue instead of just jumping into the flow of conversation.

When I did jump in, things usually ground to a halt until people could figure out what I was talking about. Either that or my quiet monotone voice went unnoticed. I didn't enjoy either of these, so I gradually learned to avoid trying to be the center of attention. It's not that I killed the urge; I still like to be the center of attention, but I don't want to have to work at it.

Those two qualities, not wanting to work very hard and enjoying being the center of attention gave me the drive to become a professional comedian. As a comic, not only am I the only one in the room with a microphone, people actually paid to hear what I say. What's even funnier is that I'm also paid to talk in schools. Did you hear me? When I was growing up, teachers punished me for talking in school. Now they pay me. I love America.

Anyway, seven years after starting school at a community college, I walked down the aisle and finally got my diploma.

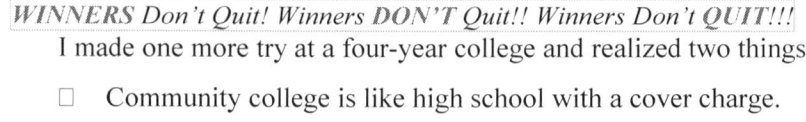

I made one more try at a four-year college and realized two things:

☐   Community college is like high school with a cover charge.

☐   Regular college was still out of reach.

Oh well, I gave it a shot. Because accounting had given me so much trouble the first time, I decided to try a three month course. Accounting, for any length of time, is tough! But I stuck it out and got an "A."

One valuable thing I learned from studying accounting was that I am not suited for work as tedious as bookkeeping. My accountant has a very nice income, but I would never want to have to do what he does. All those numbers and legal forms and tax books and the list of things I'm happier without goes on.

My webmaster and social media teacher is another important person in my life who's got a job I wouldn't want. He's great at high tech computer mumbo jumbo and he seems to love it, but leave me out of it. Just send me the bill.

As I explained before, my resistance to circumstance limited my understanding of the world. I was unwilling to see the positive side of things, and thus I couldn't spot any opportunities that would have shown me a way out.

Wherever you are and whatever you experience, try to be at peace with it. If it's hard to think positively about your situation, at least don't focus on the negatives, and instead focus on something you'd like to experience.

I have found it helpful to make a list of 1) things I'm grateful for and 2) the positive aspects of whatever I have resisted. By focusing on those aspects completely, my mind became more positive and more accepting of my circumstances.

What if we all lived our lives with a deeper and more conscious awareness of the fact that we get to create our experience of life at any moment? Wow, how cool is that? I think one word would be empowerment. Imagine what our lives, our careers and our relationships would look like if we stopped blaming our experience on ourselves, other people or on external circumstances. We would free up so much positive energy and take back so much of our personal power.

Imagine what our lives would be like if we all stopped blaming our circumstances and things and took responsibility of our own lives.

CHAPTER 7

Triumph on the Highway

Imagination is more important than knowledge.
—Albert Einstein

HAVE YOU EVER wanted something—really wanted it—and everybody said you'd never get it? One thing I really wanted during my early rehabilitation was to be able to drive again. I had to get my driver's license back. But when I asked the rehab psychologist at Harborview Hospital, he told me flat out, "Al, you'll never drive again."

So the next day, I went to the driver's retraining program at the University of Washington Hospital, and they told me the same thing. They wouldn't even let me into their program. I was furious! These guys were getting paid to help folks rehabilitate, but were they? No! I was madder than a duck without a pond. I was also more determined than ever to get my driver's license back.

But how could I? They all said I'd never drive again. I angrily gripped my cane and hobbled back to the bus stop. I slumped in the bus seat and tried to think of another way to get my license back, but I'd tried everything I could think of. Except ... but would he?

Luckily, good old Dad did come to the rescue. My father and I had been buddies since I was born. We had skied and backpacked together, and he wanted to see me get my game back. Not only that, his own father had suffered a head injury similar to mine in the First World War. I think he knew that my angry verbal outbursts would not become physical.

Like I said, I think he knew. Maybe he didn't. Anyway, my dad borrowed a neighbor's beat up Oldsmobile and handed me the keys. We went out driving. I drove all the back roads in western Washington between Everett and Renton and between Redmond and Duvall.

One day as I was leaving Redmond, red lights flashed behind me, and a siren wailed. Oh no! I pulled over to the side of the road and looked in my rear view mirror just in time to see a cop climb out of his car. He stood there for a good minute. I'm not sure, but he might have been brushing powdered sugar and donut crumbs off his shirt. Finally he came marching up to my car.

"Have you been drinking young man?"

"No. The reason I ..."

When he heard my impaired bark, the cop's eyes popped open so wide, his sunglasses almost fell off. When my dad explained what was going on—the officer was very supportive. After wishing us good luck, he sent us on our way.

About this time, I received my first small payment from the insurance company of the guy whose truck I had crashed into when he ran the stop sign. I used the money to buy a customized Datsun pickup. It was a black flatbed with dual gold wheels, oak side rails, a lockable wood tool box, smoke stacks, and the words "Born to Run"— after Bruce Springsteen's then popular album—painted on each door.

The hospital elevator had never seemed so slow. It stopped on every floor. People got on and off, some asking directions and then standing there looking confused. Finally we reached the fourth floor. I staggered out and stumbled down the hall. I breathed a prayer of thanks as I paused at one of the doors in the hallway. Knock, knock, knock…

"Come in."

I pushed the door open, hobbled in and plopped on a chair. This was going to be fun. Silently I looked at my psychologist. Finally I spoke.

"So Doc, do you think I'll ever get my driver's license back?"

"Al, we've been over this and over this. You will never drive again."

I will never forget the feelings of pride in my chest and the psychologist's stunned expression when I pulled out my new driver's license and waved it in his face. My speech therapist was right:

WINNERS Don't Quit! Winners DON'T Quit!! Winners Don't QUIT!!!

Speaking of rehabilitation or anything else, while it's true that people with life experience are likely to know what is possible, they know only averages, they don't know how much will power individuals have, and they have no way of knowing how much influence a person's higher power will exert.

CHAPTER 8

Choosing Life

Suicide is man's way of telling God, "You can't fire me—I quit.
—Bill Maher, 1995 on Politically Incorrect

WHAT IS MORE POWERFUL than our choices? Nothing! In the fall of our lives, we harvest what we planted in the spring.

Rehabilitation has been a series of choices: choosing to go to therapy, choosing to exercise between sessions, choosing to follow the advice of therapists, and most important, choosing to keep a positive Attitude.

How am I supposed to choose a positive Attitude? Choosing to look at the good that I have instead of the good I don't have is a great first step. Things seemed so dark and desperate at times that I wished I were dead. It's a good thing I was too chicken to commit suicide.

The process of rehabilitation brings about more than physical changes. It's also a process of going from a point of feeling worthless to a point of feeling like I'm on top of my game. So far, it's been a 34 year journey and it's not over yet. I still have plenty of goals, but I've also achieved plenty.

If I ever reach all my goals, what does that mean? It means my goals are too low. Reaching goals and getting regular exercise makes me feel so good about who I am that I know reaching more goals is only a matter of time.

One of the most profound lessons rehabilitation has taught me is that I choose the way I feel. For example, if I choose to talk a certain way, I will feel the way I talk. If I say negative things, I feel negative, but if I speak positively, I feel positive. I don't speak how I feel as often as I feel how I speak.

Six or seven years after my injury, the insurance company quit paying for therapy. By then I knew everything the therapist was going to have me do anyway so when a colorful newspaper ad for a local health club caught my eye, I read the whole thing. I'd belonged to the YMCA for years, but never to one of the fancier health clubs. The ad offered huge savings and pictured some great equipment the Y had not had. I used a cane, so it was evident, at least to me, that I still needed therapy. But I knew all the exercises the therapist told me to do anyway, why not spend the money that therapy would have cost on a place with nicer equipment?

Treadmills and three different kinds of stair climbing machines filled one room. The cool breeze coming from the fans washed over my back. Since I couldn't run, I put the treadmill on the steepest grade possible and, gripping the bar beside the track, I hobbled along. I felt like a disabled gerbil running on its little wheel.
After the treadmill, I tried the Nautilus equipment. Facing the huge wall mirrors around the exercise room, the chest press quickly became my favorite. Push, ease up. Push, ease up. Push, ease up.

Adrenaline flowed through my veins. Straining the non-paralyzed muscles on my right side got my endorphins firing off and going through the motions seemed to help wake up at least some of the muscles in my left arm. Pumping the weights gave me a goal and lifted my spirits so high that one night I dreamed about joining the Para-Olympics (Olympics for people with disabilities).

The dream began with me standing among a group of people with disabilities—from amputations to head injuries. The first event I was in was the boxing competition. My first opponent was a blind guy. He looked pretty tough, but I knew I could beat him. I had only one problem. Every time I punched him, his dog bit me. If I'd been thinking like a non-brain damaged person, I would have distracted the dog with a milk bone, and knocked the blind guy out. But by the time I thought of this, the match was over. Is that why they're called the Para-Olympics?

I can hear some politically correct activist saying, "That's not right! He shouldn't be talking about beating up blind guys."

Relax. It was a dream.

I've come to learn that perhaps the greatest power anyone can have is the power of choice. How we choose to see life and limits is up to us. Do I choose to see challenges or calamities? Am I a winner or a loser? For years, I didn't realize how much power I had. All I knew was I was miserable and no change was in sight. I thought my only choice was to continue suffering, or throw in my cards and experience peace.

I'd been toying with this idea ever since I came out of my coma, but I never really planned to do it. But no matter how hard I worked, things didn't get better. A long dark tunnel stretched out before me, with no light at the other end. I was like a tiny ant looking up a slippery sewer pipe, knowing there was no other way out.

After my fiancée Cheryl left me, the combination of losing her, losing other relationships, losing the material things I had—and worse—losing my ability to get them back, pushed me over the edge.

Once I made the decision, I had a sense of peace. Being able to check out gave me a feeling of power. Think how nice it would be to not have to face life with only half a body. Think how nice it would be to not have to try to function with a sluggish, forgetful, erratically undependable brain and severely unstable emotions.

Sometimes my brain would erupt with so many different ideas that while trying to figure out which one to say next, I'd forget half of what I had started to say, so my words would just kind of peter out. Even though I had complete ideas, by the time I tried to say them, I forgot what they were.

To make matters worse, my reflexes were so slow that, sometimes, by the time I verbalized my thoughts, whatever group I was trying to talk with had already changes subjects at least once or twice.

When my fiancée Cheryl, who had been my constant companion since my crash, told me our relationship was over, my worst fears came to life. How would I deal with life alone? Of course, I still had my family, thank God. But I was hungry for something a family couldn't give.

Coincidentally, at this same time, another attractive blonde who knew the family my fiancée had been staying with, came to town to stay with them for a while. She was going through a nasty divorce. We hooked up. She was broken up about her divorce and I was broken up about losing Cheryl.

At the time, it sounded like a match made in heaven. And it was… for a few weeks. But it ended in a ball of flames and burnt ashes. I went back to the choice I'd already made. The morning sun streamed through my bedroom window promising another beautiful day.

I pulled on my clothes and went down to breakfast. After eating, I went out to my flatbed Datsun pickup. It only took a few minutes to drive to the freeway overpass. I parked off the road then took out my cane and hobbled onto the bridge. I walked like a condemned man, dragging my left foot and leaning on my cane. My heart weighed a ton.

What was I doing? The idea of checking out had seemed like a massive relief at first, but the closer I got to actually doing it, the more the permanence of this solution gave me pause. Apparently I didn't want to actually die, but I wasn't ready to back out entirely. I just had to stop and think it over. I stopped in the middle of the overpass, staring down at the cars passing underneath.

I don't know how long I stood there or how long she'd been watching me, but suddenly a soft female voice broke into my thoughts.

"Hi."

"Huh?" I glanced behind me. An attractive young lady stood there.

"Do you want to talk?" I didn't say anything.

"What's wrong?" she asked.

What's wrong? Boy did I have an earful for her. It was as if someone pushed the cork into an upside down wine bottle. All the wine wanted to come out, but the cork, lodged in the bottle's neck, kept the wine from flowing freely. It just dribbled out. All my woes wanted to come pouring out, but how could I explain how it felt going from the top of the world to the pit of hell?

She must have sensed my confusion and desperation. She raised her hand, motioning to a car down the street. A patrol car drove up and stopped by the curb beside us. The attractive woman was an undercover cop! They took me to the psychiatric ward at Overlake Hospital in Bellevue, Washington.

"Wow!"

Three days in that place opened my eyes. I saw people who were so confused and mentally mixed up that I felt lucky to be me. Sure, my situation might not be ideal, but I was a lot better off than some of the folks in the psych ward. I was reminded that life isn't always a bowl of good times and happy feelings. I realized that some people see an even more dismal view of the world than I do. It's amazing how much this did to put everything in perspective.

In other words, all I had to do was open my eyes. Like they say, "Wake up and smell the coffee, Waldo!"

> **Choose Life**
>
> I can tell you things *aren't right*
>
> and that you're really *not fine*.
>
> I know you are hurting, you're breaking, you're unhappy,
>
> but I need you to stay strong and pull through
>
> because things get better and life goes on.
>
> These moments of sadness are only here
>
> to show us how wonderful the good times in life are.

Too often we underestimate the power of a touch, a kind word, a listening ear, an honest compliment, or the smallest act of caring, all of which have the potential to turn a life around. –Leo Bascaglia.

CHAPTER 9

Coping Skills

Focus on what you have, not what you don't have.
—Al Foxx

When life's problems seem overwhelming, look around and see what other people are coping with. You may consider yourself fortunate.
—Ann Landers

THE WAKE UP AND SMELL THE COFFEE, Waldo," line that ended the previous chapter was meant to emphasize the importance of our chosen perspectives. I've discovered some practical and common sense, yet easily overlooked tools, or rules of conduct that powerfully affect my circumstances and relationships. Using or not using the following tools produces either consistently positive or consistently negative results.

I didn't recognize them as anything of value when I first discovered the two behavioral tools that eventually became the most valuable in my arsenal. These tools help people around me to be comfortable and they are key in keeping me motivated and happy. I didn't discover them on my own. They were pointed out to me in not too gracious a manner.

Everything was there. If I'd had a different perspective, I could have begun using them both immediately. But as it was, only one of them was available to me. It's not like I needed to do a great deal of thinking to figure the other one out. I didn't. What I needed to do was quit thinking so much about myself and my problems.

The only reason I can give for how long it took me to do this is that I was so stuck in my self-pity mode, thinking about my horrendous circumstances and how my problems were worse than anybody else's that I seemed justified being the center of my universe. I was not yet mature enough to see the value of the gift I'd been given.

The day I was given this gift coincided with the first day I stood up out of my wheelchair and tried to walk with the use of a hemi-walker instead of one of the physical therapy room's pair of parallel bars.

I'm sitting in my wheelchair in the hall outside Harborview Hospital's physical therapy room, gripping the handle of the hemi walker in front of me and looking intently at my physical therapist that stood in front of me a few feet down the hallway. My fiancée Cheryl grips a support belt around my waist.

"OK," the therapist says. "On three, you stand up."

I stand.

"Good, move the walker forward and step up to it."

I carefully do it.

"That's great! Do it again."

I do it again.

"Beautiful! One more time…"

I do it.

"OK," she says. "Sit back down."

Sit back down? This is the first time I've stood up in months. I don't want to sit back down!

Cheryl tries to pull me back into the chair the therapist moved right behind me, but I pull away, taking a large step with my good leg. I try to follow that by stepping forward with my left leg, but that leg won't move. Down I go. I hit the hallway floor right outside my speech therapists office.

Hitting the floor stings, but not real bad. I can get up, but when I fall, Cheryl drops to her knees beside me.

"Oh, Baby, are you OK? I'm so sorry, Honey. Did you hit your head? Are you OK?"

I love attention, so I'm lying there soaking it up.

"Winners Don't Quit!" A familiar voice says. Huh? I look up. My speech therapist is standing just inside her open office door. She steps further into the hallway looking down at me.

"Don't just lie there feeling sorry for yourself. Think about everything you have.

"Half your body moves! That's more than a lot of these folks can say. *WINNERS don't quit, winners DON'T quit, winners don't QUIT* is more than a speech exercise, you have to walk your talk."

That therapist had seen too many people going through what I was to let me get away with feeling sorry for myself.

From her I learned what have become two of the most important survival tools I have. The first survival tool is rather brutish in that there is no strategy like the other tools. The first survival tool is simply, *"Winners Don't Quit!"*

The second tool I learned from my first speech therapist and from this little episode explains one reason why Winners Don't Quit. The main reason why Winners Don't Quit is because they:

> FOCUS ON WHAT THEY HAVE.
>
> NOT ON WHAT THEY DON'T HAVE.

As someone once said:

> Be thankful for what you have; you'll end up having more.
>
> If you concentrate on what you don't have,
>
> you will never, ever have enough.

CHAPTER 10

Becoming Independent

*A man has to live with himself, and he should see to it
that he always has good company.*
—Charles Evans Hughes

REGAINING MY DRIVER'S LICENSE made me redouble my
efforts to walk without a cane. I thought that if I learned to walk and
talk better, life would return to the way it had been before my accident.

I couldn't have been more wrong! My life would never be the
same. I wasn't happy until I accepted my new life and limitations, and
quit trying to recapture the old. Working hard is fine, but wasting time
and energy trying to regain something that's gone forever is not only
discouraging and self-defeating, it's just plain stupid.

For some reason, I got it in my head that living with my parents
was holding me back. I couldn't have been more wrong. I'm not sure
what made me think this way, actually I do suspect that somehow I got
the idea that Cheryl would come back to me if I proved myself capable
of living on my own.

Anyway, I got a newspaper and turned to the "Wanted to Share"
section of the classified ads. Most of the places I called hung up as soon
as they heard my speech impairment. They didn't even give me long

enough to explain why I talked the way I did. This made me mad, super mad.

I was so embarrassed by it that when my dad asked about the brevity of one such call, I told him I had called a wrong number. I vowed more than once that I'd call back and harass people who hung up on me, but I never actually called anyone back.

Writing this reminds me that I worked for several months as a telemarketer with American Handicapped Workers. Telemarketing was tough, but asking people to buy light bulbs proved easier than asking people if I could live with them. Actually, sounding like I was handicapped probably helped me sell a few more light bulbs.

Finally I found a place to live. It was an older five-bedroom house shared by five people. I was the fifth. My desire to walk without a cane really took shape and became an overpowering goal. I'd hold my cane off the ground and stagger down the sidewalk until I lost my balance, then I'd plant my cane to keep from falling. I didn't always plant it quickly enough. I fell a lot. I hit my face on the concrete a few times. Once I had to get four stitches.

I also started drinking about this time. I didn't drink for the first year after my crash, because I'd been told that drinking while taking anti-seizure medication could result in a continuing series of seizures, which would ensure that I'd never be able to drive. But that concern was over. I was off the medication and I was driving, so the logical thing to do was start drinking. The problem was that alcohol and depression go together like poor dental hygiene and cavities. The more I drank, the more depressed I got. I wasn't a daily drinker. I only drank every few days, but when I drank, I drank a lot.

Overall, I wasn't drinking as much as the four others in the house, but they were older and bigger than me and had more years of practice consuming alcohol. Plus, neither my body nor my emotions were functioning at an optimal level—even when I wasn't drunk.

To make a long and somewhat embarrassing story short, I'll just say that I was asked to move on down the road. Their distinct message ordered me to vacate the premises so quickly that the screen door couldn't hit my backside on the way out.

I never drank while I was practicing walking, I didn't have to. I walked like I was drunk without drinking. One day a red-faced man with a beer belly yelled off his porch. "Hey, guy. You're too drunk to walk. You need a designated walker."

Whatever!

Exercise was and still is a daily thing for me. I enjoy walking, but I enjoy even more exercising on the health club's exercise machines. You can't even tell I'm paralyzed when I'm sitting at one of these machines. People line up behind me to use it when I'm done. You should see how quickly they lose interest when I get up and hobble away. "I'm not using that machine. Look what it did to him."

I really like the swimming pool. I'm out there doing the one handed over hand crawl. I meet lots of people since I'm always swimming in circles.

One day I was happily swimming in my typical circle pattern and this funny feeling spread over my body. Suddenly I'm thrashing around, completely out of control. Am I having a seizure? Vaguely I'm aware of several people jumping into the pool. As it turns out, they saw me thrashing around and assumed the pool was a giant Jacuzzi. (That joke was funnier in my head. Putting it into words took the edge off.)

Over the years I began using my cane less and less, walking and limping along for greater and greater distances without it. By 1996, I was walking without it more frequently than I was using it. Today, I'm more accepting of my needs, so at the encouragement of family and friends, I use it whenever I don't need to carry something. Using my cane gives me a more stable appearance, especially if I'm hiking through the woods, a field or a crowd of people.

Physical therapy is an ongoing, intermittent, part of my life. Right now, I'm in the middle of eight therapy sessions to learn new stretching exercises designed to keep me limber so my walking continues to improve. Who knows? By the time I'm old(er) I may be able to walk without looking like I need a cane.

CHAPTER 11

Fast Cars and Bad Attitudes

The greatest discovery of my generation is that a human being can alter his life by altering his attitudes of mind.
—William James

HAVE YOU EVER FOUND IT NECESSARY to radically and suddenly adjust everything in your life?

When I moved out on my own, following my crash, my disability check was all I had for income. I soon discovered that the kind of folks I could afford to call neighbors were not exactly like the upper middle class professionals I'd grown up around. There were things like overgrown lawns, broken sidewalks, older houses with peeling paint, and down the block, an old Chevy Impala with one flat tire sat by the curb.

Maybe I should've kept living with my parents. My neighbors, however, were not my biggest problem. I was my biggest problem. If I'd known then what I know now, life would have been much easier. What do I know now that has simplified and added joy to my life and would have made my early years of rehabilitation much easier? I realize now that people avoided me because of my negative attitude. Today I know exactly what steps to take to replace a negative attitude with a positive and upbeat attitude.

You couldn't tell it from my mannerisms, but even in the day's right after my crash, I liked people and wanted friendships, but my negativity and self-pity chased them away. The kind of people who hung around me felt as bad about themselves as I felt about myself. I dealt with my negative attitude and growing depression by getting real drunk every few days. Years later I learned that alcohol treatment centers and Alcoholics Anonymous call this *binge drinking.*

The problem was that trying to cure depression by drinking is like trying to put out a fire with kerosene, drinking made me more depressed. And, without even realizing I was doing it, I'd look for and find ways to justify my depression. I found an entire list. At the top of my list of reasons to be depressed was my fiancée leaving me. Her leaving me seemed to verify the terrible way I already felt about myself. That's what really stung!

Whenever I got drunk or whenever anything happened to remind me of losing Cheryl—and it's amazing how easily I was reminded—I dove into a state of depression. One warm spring day, when I was experiencing one such depression episode, I decided to drive to the store and get some beer, but I couldn't find my keys.

Finally I grabbed my spare key, took my little pocket sized Bible and drove to a local 7-11 where I bought 3 Tall Boy cans of beer then drove a mile or so to Seattle's Green Lake where I sat in the shade, read my Bible and drank the beer.

A cute barefoot girl in cutoffs walking past where I sat saw my Bible and asked if she could sit and read the Bible with me.

My heart beat faster. "Sure, sounds good." I raised the can to my lips, but nothing came out. It was empty. No big deal. I reached in the bag for another beer, but the other two were also empty.

The girl must have noticed my disappointed expression.

"What's wrong," she asked.

"My beer's gone. I can be to the store and back in five minutes," I said, grabbing my cane and getting to my feet. "Wait here. I'll be right back."

The cool air in the 7-11 felt refreshing after the heat outside. At the beer cooler, I grabbed three more Tall Boys. The heat outside almost knocked me over when I left the store. My car felt like an oven as I backed out of the parking stall and turned toward Green Lake.

A guy in his twenties or thirties stood next to the road near the parking lot entrance with his thumb out. I asked myself "Why not? This won't take but a minute."

I stopped my car beside him. "Where you headed?"

Doubt flickered in the man's face. "I need to get up to Aurora."

"Get in," I said.

Probably my speech impairment and who knows what else made the guy pause, obviously unsure what to do.

"Hurry up!" I urged.

He got in and I quickly dropped him where he needed to go before driving back to Green Lake. After parking my car in the shaded disabled parking spot, I carried my small Styrofoam cooler across the green grass toward where I'd left the girl watching my chair and Bible.

"Hi," she said as I came close, "I'm glad you're back. I have to go now."

"Huh? OK," I said, feeling about as stupid as it's possible to feel. I'd wasted a perfectly good opportunity to make a new friend, and for what? Just because I wanted some more beer? What an idiot!

If I was depressed when I first went to Green Lake, I was even more depressed now. With all the trouble I had making friends and I passed up the opportunity to read the Bible with a cute girl who asked to read with me. Why did I have to run out of beer when I did?

What a stupid question. The question wasn't why I had to run out of beer when I did, the right question was why I thought getting more beer was more important than reading the Bible with a cute girl who asked to read with me.

I sigh in disgust at the enormous foolishness of my mistake. This opportunity's gone, but the beer isn't, and I have some bourbon back at the house. It's time to get drunk, real drunk!

CHAPTER 12

Recognizing Authority

Unthinking respect for authority is the greatest enemy of the truth.
—Albert Einstein

PERSONAL CONTROL IS what self-development is all about, and this authority is something we already possess. WE have the right to decide what is right for us and make choices, even if other people disagree.

Most people have a hard time exercising these rights because they are afraid of disapproval or loss. People with personal power spend a great deal of time looking at what they have to gain. On the other hand, people who rely on the authority of others, think about what they have to lose.

They go along to get along with other people and often resent the decisions that other people make for them. An assertive person (with their own authority) often undergoes problems at work. Although, they gain the respect of their boss, their co-workers may view them as "a butt kisser". The person who has his or her own authority appears to get away with things that other people cannot.

Are the authorities you recognize good for you? Choose carefully. It's self-destructive to let fear of something you have no control over be your authority.

Thirty years ago, during my initial years of rehab, my biggest disability wasn't my paralyzed leg and arm or my inability to control my bladder or my severe speech impairment. My biggest disability was fear: the fear of what other people thought of me. Fear was my boss. Living in fear meant I made fear my authority.

Who or what is your authority? When I used to fall frequently during my early stages of rehab, my two biggest authorities were my fear of other people thinking poorly of me and gravity. I couldn't do much to keep gravity from being my authority, but why did I allow other people's opinions to have such a disabling effect on me?

A while back, my answer would have been that I didn't have self-confidence. But that was before I realized the important role that priorities play. My priority was to have people think I'm strong and capable.

As I've grown comfortable with my disabilities, my priorities have changed. What other people think doesn't matter so much. Now my highest priority is living a useful and helpful life.

Choosing which community I will be part of and which activities I devote myself to be crucial. I either identify with the activities I engage in or become like whoever I spend most of my time with. In a sense, they become my authority.

Having healthy authorities is safe, comfortable and productive. Having the wrong authorities can waste time and be self-defeating and dangerous. I wasted a lot of time letting what other people think of me be my authority.

Fortunately, changing my priorities changed my authorities. Changing my priorities from worrying what people think to helping others required a plunge into the unknown.

This risk required supreme effort. I had to fight against my natural and cultivated tendencies. But breaking away from comfortable molds of self-concern to my new priority of caring about others freed me from worrying what people thought; my new freedoms and feelings of power gave me courage to take more risks.

Since changing who or what my authority is allows me to change my priorities, the community I'm currently choosing to identify with is key. If my chosen community has respect for things I consider honorable and worthy, continuing to associate with them helps me become happier and more content with myself and my world.

Personal authority is more than a facade. Understanding your own self-worth and willingly showing your true self is risky, yet rewarding. It is caring about how people feel without caring so much, what they think. It is being vulnerable without the need to protect your views. Even children have a personal power. In fact, the phrase "out of the mouths of babes" expresses this. It is more than innocence that makes a person unique as a child. Their personal power causes them to be open, almost fearless. You have what it takes to be the authority in your life, if you have the courage to pursue what matters to you.

Dali Lama: *"To accept that we hold the key to genuine happiness in our own hands is to discover the essential values of kindness, brotherly love and altruism. The more clearly we see the benefits of these values, the more we will reject anything that opposes them. This is how we will be able to bring about inner transformation."*

CHAPTER 13

The Clarity of Drunkenness

A drunk driver is very dangerous.
So is a drunk backseat driver, if he's persuasive.
—Demetri Martin

BACK AT THE HOUSE, I start drinking like I had a mission. As was typical, the drunker I got, the more clearly I understood how totally hopeless my life was. I could feel myself getting closer to having the courage to kill myself, what a relief that would be! Saying I was so depressed I had the courage to kill myself sounds ridiculous. Besides, I didn't want to be dead as bad as I just wanted to quit hurting. But if death was the only way I could quit hurting, then bring it on.

As happens, when a person drinks, he needs to make room for the additional liquid by letting some liquid out. On one trip to the bathroom, I saw the car keys I thought I'd lost, on the bathroom sink. I grabbed them and put them in my pocket along with my spare keys.

As I drank, I began thinking through different ways I could quit hurting. Over dosing on sleeping pills seemed like it would be the easiest, but I didn't have any sleeping pills. How about cutting my wrists? No, that's too messy, and it's gotta hurt. How about getting in a drunk-driving accident? Hey, that sounds pretty good. I could run head on into a cement truck or an 18 wheel semi.

So it was settled. I would finish off the bourbon then finish off myself.

I was way too drunk to walk without my cane. Even with a cane, my walking was so erratic that when a neighbor lady saw me staggering out to my car, she hurried over. It was a hot day, so of course I'd rolled my window down.

"Where are you going," she said coming across the front yard toward my car. "You're in no condition to drive anywhere. Come on out of the car and talk with me a while."

The invitation sounded good enough, but I remembered what happened last time a woman interfered with me when I was about to find a place where there was no more pain.

"I can't talk now" I said. "I gotta go."

"I just want to talk with you for a few minutes. Where do you have to hurry off to?"

For some reason, I felt like I had to answer her questions. In hindsight I'm not sure why I didn't just drive off. Suddenly a patrol car pulled up behind me.

She called the cops before coming out! Diving the top half of her body through my open driver's window, she grabbed my keys out of the ignition and ran back to the police car. Desperately I dug in my pocket where I'd put my spare key. What was I doing? I was too drunk to be in a car chase. Finding my spare key, I took it out and started my car.

Cars were parked on either side of the street I lived on. It seemed like I was in a parking lot. Carefully I pulled away from the curb and cautiously made my way down the street, between the rows of cars parked beside the curb on either side.

Even though I was currently going between five and ten miles an hour, the cops turned on their siren to begin the chase. I wonder how this looked to anybody watching us. My heart pounded wildly. By the time we reached the end of the block, my depression was gone.

The road at the end of the street I lived on ran parallel to the freeway. It was empty when I came around the corner, and I gave my car more gas. I sped toward a red traffic light at the end of the block.

Cars sped through the intersection I raced toward. My house was two blocks from Interstate-5. I don't know what I was thinking, but luckily I headed for the freeway—lucky because I was too drunk to go racing around narrow back streets.

Once on I-5, the race was quickly over, so I stopped. I figured they might be a bit upset, but I had no idea they'd be furious. Until that day, all I'd dealt with were courteous cops who politely handed me another ticket.

There was nothing courteous about those two cops. They stormed up to my car, and even before I could tell them that I was half paralyzed, that I was head injured, and that I was sorry, they yanked me out of my car and pushed me face down onto the street before handcuffing me and carting me off to jail!

As I slumped in the back of the patrol car during the ride in, I did some serious thinking. My depression had been taken over by my survival instinct. I had to think of a way to avoid getting a DWI. By the time we got to the police station, I had it all worked out.

It's been many years since that day, so my recollection of the exact conversation is a bit fuzzy, but I was brought into a room where they fingerprinted me and asked some questions. I put my anti-DWI plan into effect. I didn't look forward to going into another psych ward, but it beat getting a DWI and going to jail.

My not getting a DWI or any kind of ticket didn't have anything to do with the cleverness of my plan. Getting off without paying any fines or having any legal consequences had everything to do with the police officers and the court appointed psychologist recognizing that I was suicidal, trapped in circumstances beyond my control. Punishing me further wouldn't help the city, me, or them.

Until I could replace the negativity with acceptance of myself and empathy for others, I was doomed to live in a prison cell of my own making.

It took years for me to clear my head and improve my outlook and thereby my circumstances, but I still remember getting past the gate that held me in.

As long as I was getting drunk, things didn't change. They couldn't change. Change begins in your head, in your thinking. "As a man thinketh in his heart, so is he," *Proverbs 23:7.* The way I drank and the way I thought my own needs were more important than other peoples determined how I spoke and the way I spoke kept me in a prison of loneliness.

Friends are diamonds. My continuing friendship with Kathryn began one day on a city bus. I was taking a city bus to my daily vocational rehab job at Harborview Hospital. The trip from home to the hospital took two buses. Getting off one bus, I fell and sprawled across the wet sidewalk. A bit shaken, but used to frequent falls, I got up and got on the second bus.

I had barely sat in my customary place when a pretty woman a bit older than I got on the bus and asked if she could sit beside me.

"Of course," I said trying to hide my surprise. "How are you today?"

She smiled back. "Yeah it is raining hard."

"Huh?" What was she talking about, raining? She must be one of those crazy bus people.

"Shoot!" I said out loud. "I might as well be talking to my cane."

She started laughing. "I'm kidding. I just do that when I don't want to talk to anybody."

"That's funny. How often does it work?"

"Every time," she said. "I just keep it up until they quit trying to talk to me."

I laughed.

"I saw you fall," she said. "When you got right back up and kept going, just like you hadn't even fallen, I decided that, if I had the chance, I wanted to talk with you."

I fell all the time, so I hadn't even thought about it. But Kathryn noticing and wanting to talk to me just because I'd gotten back up and kept going made me feel good about myself.

We met on the bus two or three days a week for a little less than a year. We got to know each other pretty well. I told her about my therapy and she told me she was going through a divorce and custody fight.

She had an entire world of problems I'd never dreamed of. Listening to her story and being interested in her circumstances taught me more than I remember.

CHAPTER 14

Changing Limitations to Possibilities

Without leaps of imagination or dreaming, we lose the excitement of possibilities. Dreaming, after all, is a form of planning.
—Gloria Steinem

DO YOU REALIZE THE POWER of what you say? Our words shape us. Because I hated my injury, I spoke like I hated it. Negativity crowded out any positive thoughts before they could take hold. My negativity kept me from seeing the blessings I had. If you want to change your external circumstances, start by changing your internal circumstances. My negativity built on itself. It grew and grew. I had to find a way to break the cycle!

Because I was drowning in negativity, I spat out insults, profanity, and criticism. It was a vicious circle. Finally I got sick and tired of the rut I was in. I had already attempted suicide, twice, and chickened out, so I felt stuck.

Was there anything else I could do? I called mom. She would know what I should do. I didn't explain to her all the trouble I'd been in. I didn't want to cloud the issue.

Her suggestion was one I would never have thought of: "Why don't you go to Walla-Walla College where your brother is going?" Since being asked to leave Auburn Academy, I hadn't considered reenrolling in a Christian school. But I was at my wits' end. I was ready to try anything.

It was summer, so the next fall I transferred from a community college to WWC. Wow! What a great, positive experience. The positive atmosphere did me a world of good, but after a couple quarters of the easiest classes, my academic wheels began spinning like car tires on ice. I couldn't get a grip.

Walla Walla College is a great school for engineer types and people without brain damage. To quote an old cliché, I was like a fish out of water. It seemed like everybody but me knew why they were there, and they were well equipped to get the job done. I actually missed the non-demanding atmosphere of a psych ward.

I found myself studying way harder than I had at the community college. The positive atmosphere made it easier to study, but even with all my studying I was barely getting C's.

At least being in a very positive environment, I was able to free myself from the bottle. I was actually finishing classes! But alcohol is cunning, baffling and powerful, and by the third quarter, I was beginning to drink again. Just a little in the evening at first. But then I started drinking at lunchtime, then in the morning before class.

Pretty soon I was going to class drunk. Before I knew it, I was as bad as before going to Walla Walla College (WWC). Thankfully, faculty at WWC was more concerned about my welfare than the faculty at the community college.

I was told that I couldn't re-enroll until I returned to Seattle and completed an inpatient alcohol treatment program. I took their advice, completed the program, and when I re-enrolled at WWC, I was clean and sober. I thought I'd do better at my studies now that I had stopped drinking. But other difficulties emerged. I'd already taken the easier classes. The remaining ones were a lot tougher. World History was my undoing. The required reading was drudgery, but I hung in there and finished every page.

Things would have been fine, if I hadn't been expected to understand and remember what I'd read. Yeah right. Like a crammed hard drive, my brain was passing its maximum capacity just doing the reading.

Trying to actually understand and recall what I read was asking too much. I kept trying to finish my studies at Walla- Walla College, but I couldn't keep my grades high enough and financial aid was no longer an option. I left Walla-Walla College and finished my two year degree at Seattle Central Community College.

I didn't seem capable of learning and retaining enough of what I'd learned to graduate from more than a community college. Holding down a job with the skills I learned in college was a dream. Looking back, the most important lesson college taught me was the value of getting along well with people. But re-learning this lesson was tricky.

As a teenager, I had always gotten along well with people. But trying to relate normally to people now had become a real challenge. With a ruptured hypothalamus, a shattered short term memory, slow understanding, and an intermittent personality state that included anger and depression, you might understand what I was up against.

If it hadn't been for a major change in my outlook, things would still be the same. I would have continued seeing calamities instead of challenges. I would have continued to be a depressed fountain of negativity. Then, through a string of insights and realizations, my outlook changed.

One key realization allowed me to change my perceptions and change my life, that realization was that I didn't have things any worse than a lot of people. This realization set me free to begin seeing possibilities instead of limitations.

CHAPTER 15

Importance of Spirituality

*In modern times spirituality has been separated from religion,
and denotes a blend of humanistic psychology with mystical and esoteric
traditions and eastern religions aimed at personal well-being and
personal development.* —Wikipedia

*Spirituality I take to be concerned with those qualities of the human spirit,
such as love, compassion, patience, tolerance forgiveness,
a sense of responsibility, a sense of harmony
which brings happiness to both ourselves and others?*
—His Holiness, the Dalai Lama

BEING ABLE TO ACCEPT LIFE, with its countless details, as moving along exactly as it should--may seem like the ultimate utopia. What could be more peaceful and less free of concern than believing that everything is going along exactly as it should? Accepting life on life's terms seems the goal of every eastern and western religion.

For me, accepting life on life's terms includes accepting that my physical condition is exactly what it's supposed to be right now. Although half my body remains paralyzed and my cancer diagnosis and operation will carry lifelong scars, doing what I can to keep my mind and body as alert and in as good of shape as possible is vital to experiencing the peace that comes with acceptance.

A place that strongly advocates acceptance of life's challenges and keeping as physically and spiritually healthy as possible is Weimar

Institute, a self-supporting seminary and health care center in Weimar, California. Since 1978 Weimar Institute has pioneered a modern-day implementation of a school that incorporates health, evangelism and work education along with strong academics. Their Core of Four include praying, studying and working to develop new ways of integrating their key characteristics of education to a higher level. Further, they valued other methods of education, including manual labor skills and other innovative ways to meet the mental and physical as well as spiritual needs.

Left to my own devices, becoming a student at Weimar Institute is not something I would have chosen to do. But my being asked to leave two prior Christian schools disappointed my parents and made me want to do something to make them proud and to restore their faith in me. Weimar Institute is an amazing place, for people who are not rule breakers by nature. I could see value in living the life promoted by the institute, and I really tried to follow the rules and live according to how they want their students to live.

One of the first things I noticed at the institute is that they have a life style program that's separate from the seminary and high school that diabetics come to from all over the world. I watched former diabetics quit needing to rely on insulin after participating in Weimar Institute's 30 day, health restoring program. I didn't have diabetes but I didn't always speak as positively as it is to my benefit to speak, and my thoughts of life were not as healthy as it could have been.

The **NEWSTART** acronym I learned at Weimar is part of the health program and it helps me get the most out of life I can. I use this acronym to keep physically fit and that supports maintaining my positive attitude. Although we're in control of our attitudes, sometimes we need to have more than control, we also need to have strategies and directions. Building a strong and positive attitude is like building a house or a model car. It helps to have a plan, a set of directions.

The **NEWSTART** acronym is the first part of my formula for living a life of happiness, peace and spiritual fulfillment:

Nutrition	Eat plenty of nutritious food.
Exercise	Exercise to increase strength and stamina.
Water	Drink plenty of water.
Sunlight	Get plenty natural light—go outside!
Temperance	Live a temperate lifestyle.
Air	Get plenty of good, fresh outside air.
Rest	Get enough sleep to feel well-rested.
Trust	Trust that your inner spiritual beliefs give needed strength.

When I discipline myself to live according to the NEWSTART acronym, I feel better about myself. The better I feel about myself, the better I feel about others and the better I feel about life in general. And the better I feel about life, the more optimistic I am. When I'm feeling optimistic, it's much easier to believe in possibilities.

Since believing in possibilities actually creates possibilities, it's clear that living according to the **NEWSTART** acronym by taking care of myself both physically and spiritually, is the best way to be healthy and happily productive.

As helpful as the **NEWSTART** acronym is, it is not the end all and be all. There are other helpful sources of strength and a correct focus, especially if you're addicted to substances or self-serving thought and behavior patterns. Alcoholics Anonymous has been for me a source of wisdom and a spiritual refuge.

I continued going to meetings, attending two meetings a week during my first two years at Weimar Institute. Good as the principles were that I was learning at the institute, they couldn't take the place of the truths built-in to the AA program. There's a principle that's central to AA that addresses the needs of an addict without interfering with what they're learning from whatever other spiritual group they are part of. A paraphrase of that principle follows:

> The purpose of AA is not to get us to heaven, or keep us from hell, but to keep us sober long enough to decide where we want to go.

Although the Christian schools I attended until I was asked to leave claimed to have the Truth about God, the problem with the God I met in school and church was that that God was the God of someone else's understanding. This is a fine and necessary part of getting acquainted with God, but until I had a God of my own understanding, I didn't have an internal shift in my thinking that consequently changed my behavior. When I gained a God of my understanding, my thinking shifted into more of a live and let live mode.

Like most people, I tend to make the same choices as whatever group I'm currently choosing to hang around. As long as I continued going to AA, following the rules and benefitting from the positive atmosphere at Weimar Institute was an easy pleasure. My problem came when I decided that since I was living at Weimar Institute where I was never tempted to do the things AA gave me the resolve to not do, I didn't need to go to AA.

The problem with thinking this way is that mind altering substances are everywhere! And they are cunning, baffling and powerful. In the nearly two years I'd been at Weimar Institute, I had seen no signs of that sort of thing. I felt perfectly safe in ending my AA attendance.

Another lesson my journey taught me is: Don't make assumptions! Within a month of feeling safe quitting going to AA, a fellow pastoral ministry major asked me if I would like to smoke some pot with him. Huh? I've asked myself a million times why I did it.

The answer is clear. Not having regular attendance at AA to keep my thinking in check, memories of past good times crowded out the memories of where my addictive nature would eventually take me and I said: "Sure! Let's do it." That choice ended my Weimar adventure and sent me on a detour that wasted more than a decade.

I'm back in AA now and am within two years of having double digit sobriety. Because of how much better life works when I'm clean and sober, I feel sure I will not let anything keep me from the clear minded blessings that seem to come when I'm regularly attending AA meetings. Regularly attending AA meetings helps keep my attitude where it needs to be. My belief is not only in the power of my attitude but in the power of trusting in a higher power.

Here is a prayer asking to be a better soul. It's impossible for me to repeat that prayer and not feel better; somehow it recalibrates me.

> Lord, make me an instrument of your peace. Where there is hatred, let me sow love. Where there is injury, pardon. Where there is doubt, faith. Where there is despair, hope. Where there is darkness, light. Where there is sadness, joy. O Divine Master, grant that I may not so much seek to be consoled, as to console; to be understood, as to understand; to be loved, as to love. For it is in giving that we receive. It is in pardoning that we are pardoned, and it is in dying that we are born to Eternal Life. Amen.
>
> ~St. Francis of Assisi

There is no one "right" way to grow. See what is beautiful in every religion, and in every belief system. Honor other people's paths even if they are different from yours. Be inclusive & loving, and look beyond the form of people's beliefs to the essence. There is no right way; there is only the way that is right for you.

Regardless of the spiritual or religious tradition adhered to; everyone I know desires a feeling of well-being. And if they're like most of the people I know, they also like to know they are developing into better people.

CHAPTER 16

The Power of Words

The words 'I am' are potent words; be careful what you hitch them to.
The thing you're claiming has a way of reaching back and claiming you.

—A. L. Kitselman

FIFTEEN YEARS AFTER MY CRASH, I somehow got accepted into Western Washington University. Interestingly enough, I started doing standup comedy that same year.

All my university experience did was to confirm my academic limitations. Brain damage and poor study skills still held me in their grip. Even tutors didn't help, but my comedic endeavors proved to be much more positive.

Do you like being on stage? Are we ever really off stage? The stage lights hid the audience, but I knew they were there. I accepted the microphone the mc handed me and spoke into it. "Wow! Was he hot or what? Where'd those cards come from?" The audience applauded wildly at the comments I made about the magician who had gone before me.

The magic man had seemed to "speak" cards, as well as coke bottles and bananas into and out of existence. In a way, his act was a lot like life. We're all magicians, but only a few of us realize the magical power our words have.

It's amazing to me that I took so long to see the correlation between what I said and what happened to me. I was like a magician— the more I said negative things, the more anger and depression popped out of the hat. When I finally became aware of this, years before this, I spoke with my psychologist about it, and I started reading books on the subject.

I gradually realized that I had made a life-changing discovery. I had discovered that my words—anyone's words—are like magic. Our words have the power to tear us down or build us up. Our words can tear others down or build them up. Whether we see ourselves as winners or losers determines how we talk. And how we talk determines whether we are winners or losers.

Winners can afford to build people up. Losers spend their time tearing others down, to feel better about themselves. The problem with tearing people down to build yourself up is that you begin to feel contempt for yourself. The beauty is that when you say and do things to build people up—when you smile, listen, encourage, recognize, and sincerely appreciate others—you feel worthwhile yourself.

We can choose whether we want to be a winner or a loser. Being a winner or a loser determines how we choose to see our life's circumstances. Do we choose to see obstacles or opportunities? Do we choose to speak about our victories or our failures? It's up to us.

Changing how I spoke, so I spoke like a winner instead of a loser, took me a long time for two reasons. One reason was the company I kept. I hung around people who spoke negatively. The second reason was because the negative words I kept speaking made me think negatively. Our words have incredible power over ourselves and others.

Some people believe that you speak the way you feel. That's only half-correct. How we feel is as much a result of how we speak, as how we speak is a result of how we feel. Sounds circular, right? That's because it is. I know from my experience and that of others, that we don't speak the way we feel as often as we feel the way we speak.

The next time you are feeling low, try saying only cheerful, positive things to folks. You will soon begin feeling better. As the old saying goes--*"Fake it 'till you make it."*

An image I use in some of my talks is this. Picture everyone having an imaginary bucket hanging around their neck. The bucket holds that person's self-esteem. Each time I do or say something that hurts them, I punch a hole in their self-esteem bucket.

At the same time I puncture their bucket, I puncture my own bucket. Every time I do something to help the person fill his or her bucket, I fill my own bucket with increased self-esteem. Following my crash, my greatest need was to rebuild my confidence. My poor self-image contributed to my social problems.

I began asking psychologists how to feel better about myself, and I paid particular attention to things that filled my self-esteem bucket. If we all realized how much our self-esteem buckets fill up when we fill other people's buckets, there would be bucket brigades everywhere.

Because the things I say have the power either fill or poke holes is someone else's self-esteem bucket, what I say can either create opportunities or destroy possibilities. Faced with the choice to be a creator or a destroyer, I choose to be a creator.

There is no one "right" way to grow. See what is beautiful in every religion, and in every belief system. Honor other people's paths even if they are different from yours. Be inclusive & loving, and look beyond the form of people's beliefs to their essence.

CHAPTER 17

Filling Your Self-Esteem Bucket

In my day, we didn't have self-esteem, we had self-respect,
and no more of it than we had earned.
—Jane Haddam

AS SOON AS I OPENED MY MOUTH and asked the woman behind the grocery stores cash register how much a Snickers bar cost, I could tell from her expression that there would be a problem.

"Pardon me?" she said in a slightly louder voice than was necessary.

"How much is one of these?" I asked holding up a candy bar. I carefully enunciated each word, and I know she understood me; she must have. She answered me! Slowly and loudly enough for everybody behind me in line to hear, she said, **f-i-f-t-e-e-n c-e-n-t-s.**

I scowled and loudly said, "**T—h—a—n—k, y—o—u!**"

It got a few laughs, but episodes like this drained my self-esteem. Why did that cashier have to embarrass me? Why did I have to react like I had? My actions called more attention to the embarrassing situation than hers had.

Normally I wouldn't have even remembered the event, but in this situation, my hot headed reaction really bothered me. I needed to stop letting what people might be thinking about me have so much power over how I felt about myself.

I remembered the last time something like this happened. I had reacted well, and my response had made me feel good. It happened when I was practicing walking around the big block I lived on.

The best thing about living in the big old house on the hill was the nice wide sidewalk that went all the way around the block. The block was rectangular, with the long sides of the rectangle going up and down the hill. One short side of the rectangle was at the top of the hill and the other was at the bottom.

One day I came hobbling up the hill, holding my cane aloft as I would do until I lost my balance and had to plant my cane and catch myself. I must have looked quite the sight staggering up the sidewalk with my cane in the air. One time a neighbor called off his porch,

"Are you all right young man?"

I was too focused on what I was doing to stop and answer him, so without stopping or even looking I said, "Oh yeah, I'm fine." I didn't hear everything the old guy said before he went back inside and the screen door slammed shut, but it was something about "drunken belligerents."

The doctors said I'd never walk without a cane, but I had to walk without a cane. It wasn't about not liking to be told I couldn't do something. I didn't like being told I couldn't do something any more than the next guy, and I wasn't thinking about proving someone wrong. I was only thinking about not settling for anything less than the most I could do.

I held my cane off the ground and hobbled around the block. Every time I started to fall, I'd plant my cane and try to catch myself. Sometimes I missed.

I fell so much in those days that I actually got used to it, but I hated to fall in public. I hated for people to feel sorry for me. I remember one day I had a particularly bad fall.

A young woman and her young son were walking behind me. Well, it was probably her son. Anyway, they stopped and the woman said, "Are you OK, sir? Can we help you?"

Trying to sound cheerful, like nothing was wrong, I said, "Oh, yeah. I'm fine."

When the woman heard my garbled response, she looked stunned. She grabbed the child's hand. "Come on Billy. He's drunk."

They hurried off up the hill. I scrambled to my feet and followed after them, holding my cane off the ground and repeating the speech exercise my speech therapist had given me.

WINNERS Don't Quit! Winners DON'T Quit!! Winners Don't QUIT!!!

Whether I'm speaking to store clerks, practicing my walking or working on marketing my speaking business to include everyone from fortune 500s to various non-profits, how many times I have to repeat myself, how many mistakes I make or how many times I fall doesn't matter nearly as much as how I respond to failing. All that really matters is how many times I get back up and keep trying.

In the movie "I am Sam", the main character, Sam, is an adult with a developmental disability. An initially insensitive attorney says to Sam: I need that list of names from you—people who can testify that you're a good father despite your handicap. I didn't mean your handicap, I meant your disability [shakes her head]--The fact that you're retarded. That's not the right word [exasperated]. I don't know what to call you!

To which he replies: "Sam. You can call me Sam."

CHAPTER 18

Adapting to Change

The time to make up your mind about people is never.
—Grace Kelly

ACCEPTING PEOPLE, PLACES AND THINGS helps people transform themselves so they can adapt to challenging *changes*, so their attitudes flow like an easy stroll on a pleasant Sunday morning. People who have not learned the power of *changing* their attitudes by accepting and adapting are likely to have attitudes that have to be weathered like unpleasant storms.

I don't happen to like excessively cold weather, especially when snow starts sticking to the streets. (Snow should stay in the mountains and on post cards where it belongs.)

If you're like me and live in a part of the country, like Seattle, that experiences more rain than snow, when it snows, the lack of familiarity and preparation makes snow dangerous to drive in.

And if you limp and are prone to falling when it's snowy and icy, as I do, then you can probably understand that it's easy for me to dislike both driving and walking in the stuff. This is where an attitude of acceptance and adaptability works and is beneficial for all concerned.

This first time this became evident to me was when my dear friend Bonnie told me that she loves the snow. She lived in a ski resort for many years and participated in all the winter sports. She said that hearing me complain about the snow and winter weather made her enjoyment of the snow and winter weather difficult. She said that I took the joy away.

Because my relationship with Bonnie is more important to me than the weather, I *changed* my attitude and adapted. I just dress warmer, use my cane, and am more aware of my comments. Manning up my attitude seemed like a more attractive option than complaining about something I could not *change*. Accepting snow is good practice for other things I cannot *change*.

Live and let live. Why should we waste our energy complaining about things we can't *change*? Choose your attitudes about weather and other issues carefully. Acceptance of things outside you starts with accepting yourself. When I'm operating from a foundation of self-acceptance, it's easier to transform myself by adapting my attitude so I avoid unnecessary conflicts.

Burned Biscuits: Bonnie shared the following story with me. It is a perfect example of acceptance in its highest form.

When I was a kid, my mom liked to make breakfast food for dinner every now and then. One night, she made breakfast after a long, hard day at work. She served us biscuits and gravy, complete with eggs and sausage. She placed a plate of eggs, sausage and extremely burned biscuits in front of my dad. I remember wondering what he would do.

He reached for his biscuit, smiled at my mom and asked me how my day was at school. I don't remember what I said, but I do remember watching him smear butter and jelly on that ugly burned biscuit. He ate every bite of that thing... never made a face nor said anything!

> When I got up from the table that evening, I remember Mom apologizing to Dad for burning the biscuits.
>
> I'll never forget him saying: "Honey, I love burned biscuits every now and then."
>
> Later that night, I went to kiss Daddy good night and I asked him if he really liked his biscuits burned. He wrapped me in his arms and said, "Your Momma put in a hard day at work today and she's real tired. And besides - a little burned biscuit never hurt anyone!"

I've thought about this story many times. Life is full of imperfect things and imperfect people. I'm not the best at anything, except perhaps making the best oatmeal you will ever have. I often forget birthdays and anniversaries, just like everyone else. What I have learned is that accepting each other's imperfections, and choosing to celebrate each other's differences, is a key to creating lasting relationships.

And that's my prayer for you today -- that you will learn to take what you understand as the good, the bad, and the ugly parts of what other people say or do and realize that neither you nor anybody else is perfect. This understanding is essential to being part of a relationship where a burnt biscuit isn't a deal-breaker!

Understanding is the base of any relationship, husband-wife, parent-child or friendship: "Don't give the key to your happiness to someone else - keep it, and be happy." Please pass me a biscuit. Yes, the burned one will *be just fine.*

I'm not saying that life is about winning and losing attitude battles. It's not! Life is about *adjusting* your expectations and your tolerance so you can accept the good, the bad, and the ugly parts of people, so you both feel like winners.

Childhood Wisdom: The three year old kindergartner stood just inside my peripheral vision, but I was too focused on coloring with the children sitting at the round table to really see him. The kids had challenged me. They didn't think I could color as well as a girl who was their reigning coloring champion.

"Can I sit on your knee?" the three-year old finally asked. Several other kindergartners and I sat around the table. I felt completely accepted! I love the attitude children have. They didn't adjust how they spoke to me when they heard my speech impairment. Most of them sounded like they had speech impairments, too. Why do we lose the attitude of a child?

It had been about two years since my crash, and the time I spent volunteering with children were the safest times I knew. They never acted like they thought I was mentally impaired. They never pretended they didn't see me. They couldn't always understand me, but that's OK. I didn't always understand them either.

Changing my expectations of myself helped me go from being a physically active teen with one life to a physically impaired person with a completely different, though satisfying life. I never felt as accepted and approved of as when a child wanted to sit on my lap or include me in their coloring contests.

A pastor that spent time with me during this period of my life had two children, a boy and a girl. I think his name was Pastor Mike Brown, but it's been 30 years or more, so I could be way wrong.

Anyway, I remember, like it was yesterday, how I taught the younger of the two to say the alphabet. And I taught the older one to read a few simple words. Mike was amazed, or at least he did a convincing job of acting amazed. The important thing is my memory of the joy I felt at teaching and interacting with those kids.

The beauty of children is their honesty. They say it like they see it. And they see it with the purity of innocence. They don't have any preconceived ideas. They don't have plans or schemes or ulterior motives. They live in the now, and they express themselves freely.

My head injury reduced me to the mental age of an infant. When a child expresses themselves freely, it's called cute. Temper tantrums, of course, are not seen in quite the same light. But, hopefully for the most part, parents simply roll their eyes or blush at some of the things their child says. What else can they do?

But when a grown man behaves with a childlike innocence, I can say from personal experience that he is seen as an immature irritant nobody wants to hang around.

Although it's been long enough since my head injury occurred for me to have grown up and become more mature in my thinking, my best friend Bonnie says I've managed to hang on to some childlike tendencies, like what she identifies as "my innocence" and the occasionally unearned trust I give to people.

She says "they're cute," but I'm given to missing sarcasm and believing things are the way I want them to be. In other words, I'm fairly gullible. So I'm trying to figure out if cute means adorable, immature or a little of both. I wouldn't mind being a little of both.

Changing Like a River: Have you ever seen a raging river cascading down a mountain, racing through a channel dug into the very rock? Finally it splashes into a bowl it's dug at the mountain's base. From there, it begins a gentle flow across the surrounding prairie. Rivers have an amazing ability to *change*, to adapt to the land. In many ways, each of us is like a river. We too must adapt and keep flowing, keep moving.

But how do we adapt to horrendous challenges?

In a word, acceptance! Accept the world on the world's terms, like the rivers do. A river doesn't let a rock or a tree trunk stop it. It adapts, going over, under or around them, flowing to its final destination.

Adaptability is the key. Just like a river faces obstacles and keeps on flowing, we also must face obstacles, troubles, disappointments, pains and keep flowing. Or like a young child who falls. They just get up and keep going like nothing happened.

After my paralyzing motorcycle crash, I faced obstacles and other *changes* no teenager or individual wants to face. I could not talk, could not walk, and could not drive. I didn't want to be paralyzed, a vegetable plucked from the garden of life. Adapting to my *changed* condition was harder than the condition itself.

The key to adapting is accepting. Accepting was the hardest, and the most helpful lesson I've ever learned. Like a river that continues to flow day and night, years of rehabilitation reawakened my spirit and my life began flowing again as I learned to accept my situation.

The recovery I've gained is in proportion to my willingness to accept my condition and flow with it. When I accept what life offers, my life flows. And just as rivers flow toward a final destination like the ocean, acceptance of ourselves and of others allows us to create and flow toward our destiny of love and happiness.

Acceptance, the act of bringing inner peace, often changes the outer reality we had to accept. The person we disagreed with, once he feels accepted, may become a trusted friend. The challenge of a difficult new job, once accepted, may lead to a long and satisfying career. Even acceptance of a Toastmaster assignment can lead to an advancement of our poise and confidence.

CHAPTER 19

Believing In Myself

You'll see it when you believe it.
—Wayne Dyer

You yourself, as much as anybody in the entire universe,
deserve your love and affection.
— Siddhārtha Gautama

EVERY NOW AND THEN I did receive a dose of encouragement. The family my fiancée lived with was always supportive. The husband suffered a head-injury years before.

"You've done so well, Al. Your parents must be awfully proud of you," Betty, his wife, would say. She was always saying positive things to me.

I shrugged, "Yeah. They're proud. Who can blame 'em?" I laughed. Making little jokes whenever people complimented me was easier than acknowledging the compliment. Since I didn't believe the positive things people said about me, it was hard for me to accept compliments. I didn't feel good about myself, so I didn't really believe anyone else did either.

And the habit of self-deprecation, it turns out, has damaging side effects: People who default to self-deprecating comments are more likely to exhibit low self-esteem. When we repeat a behavior again and again, it starts to form neural pathways in your brain and pretty soon you start to change the way you think about yourself.

I thought people said nice things to me because they felt sorry for me. During the initial years after my accident, people complimented me and frequently told me they admired all the hard work I was doing. This would have boosted my self-esteem, if I'd believed them.

But how could I believe them? I saw myself as pathetic, someone to be pitied, not someone deserving respect or admiration. As I mentioned, during this time if I received a positive compliment, I'd laugh and shrug it off.

When it comes to building self-confidence, I learned perception is everything. The way I viewed myself had a huge impact on how others ultimately perceived me. There may be some factors beyond our control when it comes to the confidence game, but we're in the driver's seat, holding the keys to our public persona.

What was unfortunate about this time is that when someone said something negative or derogatory about me, I latched onto it and made it part of my self-belief. This was something I could identify with because it was what I already believed about myself.

In other words, all my accomplishments, all the goals I reached, and limits I overcame did not fill my self-esteem bucket because of the negative way I thought and spoke about myself. Speaking positively to myself and others about myself and others is one of the most important things I can do to raise my self-esteem.

No one is perfect the first time out, but often self-confidence teeters on a mountain of goals and expectations. If we get rattled when we aren't the best at something or when things don't go according to plan, we'll always be at the mercy of factors we can't control.

When we lack confidence, it's easier to stay with the familiar. Real confidence-boosting power comes from tackling something new, though. We may not succeed right away, but when we do, the experience is liberating. Many people never achieve their full potential -- not because the opportunities aren't out there, but because they're afraid to risk failure.

Think of it this way: If we aren't taking risks, we aren't growing as a person. When we fail at a new challenge, it's a sign we're getting somewhere. It's one more mistake we won't make again.

There's an extra added bonus, too. Developing self-confidence is a process, and once we've worked through the fear of failing, it gets easier. You know you'll survive the humiliation of revealing your imperfect self, and you'll begin to realize that a few initial failures are a small price to pay for learning and experiencing new things.

When it comes to building self-confidence, perception is everything. The way you view yourself has a huge impact on how others will ultimately perceive you. There may be some factors beyond your control when it comes to the confidence game, but you're in the driver's seat, holding the keys to your public persona.

Here are sixteen powerful activities I've discovered for filling my bucket with self-esteem and genuine confidence.

Thankfully, there are a number of simple things that anyone can do to boost his or her self-esteem and, hopefully, break out of this vicious circle. You may already be doing some of these things, and you certainly don't need to do them all. Just do those that you feel most comfortable with.

1. Make three lists: one of your strengths, one of your achievements, and one of the things that you appreciate about yourself. Try to get a friend or relative to help you with these lists. Keep the lists in a safe place and read through them regularly. My strength is my sense of humor, my accomplishment was becoming an award winning comic, and what I appreciate about myself is that I forgive easily.

2. Think positively about yourself. Remind yourself that, despite your problems, you are a unique, special, and valuable person, and that you deserve to feel good about yourself. Identify and challenge any negative thoughts that you may have about yourself, such as 'I am a loser', 'I never do anything right', or 'No one really likes me'. Being brain damaged has sometimes made me feel that I have less to contribute than other people who obviously are not brain damaged. However, I have to honestly say that there are a lot of people out there that seem brain-damaged even though they are not. I focus on that I am as smart as most people, I just have to keep things simple and organized for me to function well.

3. Pay special attention to your personal hygiene: every day may be the day you meet someone who you are very interested in impressing. Always look your best. First impressions matter. Of course this includes all the different types of personal care you would expect a professional person to do. For example, unless you're a flamenco guitarist, a squirrel who needs added traction while climbing trees or are going for a Guinness World Record, keep your nails neatly trimmed.

4. Dress in clothes that make you feel good about yourself. This is an area that I have not been very good at. My best friend has been very helpful helping me to find clothes that make me look professional and comfortable. I also have a collection of Boston derby hats that is like no other. Please don't ask me how many I have…

5. Eat good food as part of a healthy, balanced <u>diet</u>. Make meal times a special time, even if you are eating alone. Turn off the TV or radio, set the table, and arrange your food so that it looks attractive on your plate. Growing up in a home where my mother was a nurse and my father who worked for the State Food and Drug Administration, healthy eating was drilled into my mind. I grew up vegetarian and have integrated several servings of meant into my diet each week.

6. Exercise regularly: go out for a brisk walk every day, and take more vigorous exercise (exercise that makes you break into a sweat) three times a week. I belong to the YMCA and have exercise equipment at my home. I do 100 push-ups every day (in 2 – 3 sets), even with one viable arm and hand. If there is a will, there is a way.

7. Ensure that you are getting enough <u>sleep</u>. I would do better on this if it wasn't for the late night talk show addiction I seem to have. Oh well, everyone has their cross to bear.

8. Manage your <u>stress</u> levels. I remind myself of everything that's good in your life by focusing on what I have, not what I don't have.

9. Do more things that you enjoy doing. I try to do at least one thing that I enjoy every day, and remind myself that I deserve it.

10. Get involved in activities such as painting, music, poetry, and dance. For me, I have learned how to play a harmonica. I'm not real good like my father, but when we play together, it is great!

11. Set yourself a challenge that you can realistically achieve, and then go for it! It was my goal to be a good driver. Am I a good driver? Not as good as I could be, but at least I have a license saying I'm legal. And I don't have to take the bus or rely on others to shuttle me around. The harder I try to reach a goal, the more my self-esteem bucket is filled, even if I don't reach the goal completely. If I reach every goal the first time I try, my goals are too easy.

12. Do some of the things that you have been putting off, such as clearing out the garden, washing the windows, or filing the paperwork. Working on my paperwork, filing, making lists are all things I do to make my life more organized, allowing me to feel good that I'm getting it done.

12. Do something nice for others. For example, strike up a conversation with the person at the till, visit a friend who is sick, or get involved with a local charity. I love to talk with people, at the grocery store, at my bank, with people in the waiting room of a doctor's office... Visiting sick friends has been fulfilling. When I do something kind for others, it makes me feel good about myself. And I find myself at fundraisers, generally as a keynote speaker.

14. Being friendly and outgoing: I'm pretty friendly. I could make friends with a rock. I wasn't always like that, but if you don't stand out in a positive way when you have a disability, you will be left in the dust. I do warn you to be conscience of other people's circumstances in regard to their ability to be able to socialize freely. If they are working, be sure not to interfere with their need to get their work done. Sometimes our loneliness or need to connect with others can misguide our good intensions. Our friendliness will be more effective if it's about what we can do for others, rather than what others can do for us.

15. Have a close friend or two that you can confide in, but do not share your problems with everyone you know. Most people have their own things to worry about. Being too willing to share your problems can cause people to regret seeing you coming. Remember that you have things to be thankful for. Be more willing to share these things than things that are a problem for you. The more you share the positive, the more positive you'll get receive.

Try to spend more time with those you hold near and dear. At the same time, try to enlarge your social circle by making an effort to meet people. I belong to Toastmasters and meet very nice people who desire to learn the best ways to communicate as speakers. We all learn from each other and I find it great fun. And I regularly spend time with my parents, who are always supportive and kind and uplifting for me.

When life doesn't quite turn out the way we expect it will or want it to, we need to give ourselves a little wiggle room. Self-confidence is a powerful characteristic to cultivate. The more we reward ourselves for stepping out of our comfort zone and trying something new instead of bashing ourselves for a less-than-stellar performance, the easier it will be to tackle the next challenge with confidence.

Most people's thoughts and feelings about themselves fluctuate somewhat based on their daily experiences. The grade we get on an exam, how our friends treat us, ups and downs in a romantic relationship can all have a temporary impact on how we feel about ourselves.

Our self-esteem, however, is something more fundamental than the normal ups and downs associated with situational changes. For people with good self-esteem, normal ups and downs may lead to temporary fluctuations in how they feel about themselves, but only to a limited extent. In contrast, for people with poor self-esteem, these ups and downs drastically impact the way they see themselves.

Healthy self-esteem is based on our ability to assess ourselves accurately and still be accepting of who we are. This means being able to acknowledge our strengths and weaknesses (we all have them!) and at the same time recognize that we are worthy and worthwhile.

CHAPTER 20

The Company We Keep

The five people that you spend most of your time with
will dictate how far your life and career will go.
—Will Smith

"YOU ARE WHAT YOU EAT. YOU ARE WHAT YOU WEAR."
But what about who you know? Each of us has their reserved set of cultural and spiritual set of values, opinions, expressions and emotions, but it is an indisputable fact that our quality of life is a direct reflection of the company we keep.

What is the measure of a person? Are we based solely on our accomplishments? Or do the bonds and relationships we form play a part in who we ultimately become? I gravitate toward the latter, which states that I am what/who I surround myself with. Our friends, colleagues, and significant others all play a part in how we carry ourselves as well as how we are perceived by the world at large.

You are what you surround yourself with. The mantra couldn't be any-more simple. It is apparent in everything: our quality of life, the way we articulate ourselves, the way we dress, even the women (or men) we are attracted to. These are all a direct reflection of the company you keep.

One of the greatest influences in a person's life is provided by their closest friends. This is the core group of people with whom we choose to spend our free time. The sole group of people that we allow ourselves to let down your guard around and turn all defenses off. These are the people that subconsciously affect our ambition and motivation as we journey through life.

Our friends can also be toxic as well. Have you ever noticed how some people just seem to enjoy being miserable? Obviously, I'm not referring to friends that fall on troubled times, as we all do occasionally. Good friends do help one another when crisis strikes and misfortune befalls us. Here I'm referring to those individuals that can find disaster in winning the lottery *–just think of all those taxes you would have to pay!*

Some folks just cannot be cajoled, badgered or counseled out of a negative attitude about life and *everything* in it! If you have many friends like this, be aware of how this affects your mood, too. If you find, as many do, that this negativity has a *wearing* effect on your attitude, you may want to consider the company you keep.

If your friends are all driven, ambitious and creative individuals, then that rubs off on you and gets your imagination working in new and wonderful ways you may have never envisioned.

Watching those around us grow is conducive to inspiring personal growth and reinforces our desire to achieve our goals. Show me any individual's best friends and then analyze the dynamic between them. From this alone, you'll be able to easily understand who they are.

For one, we will always be judged by the company that you keep. We may not be aware of how their characteristics affect us, but the damage has been done. Naturally, others personalities will rub off on us too.

If we strive to surround ourselves with motivationally driven people, we, in turn, will become motivationally driven. Don't surround yourself with those who have ceased to proceed forward. It's much easier to progress as a group than to try to make it on your own.

When comedy club audiences laughed at a joke, I kept it. If they didn't laugh, I either change it until they did laugh, or I quit using it. I'm not the only one who's influenced by other people. We all are. Not only are we influenced by others, we imitate them.

The law of averages is a lay term to describe the statistical probability of something happening and it doesn't lie because it is based on mathematics. "The theory illustrates that the result of any given situation will be the average of all outcomes."

In sales, this law teaches us that if we want to double or triple our sales revenue that we need to double or triple qualified prospects. This law can also be applied successfully in many areas of our lives — including relationships. Meaning that you should go in for (surround yourself with) more of what you actually want in your life to heighten your chances of attaining it.

For example, if we continue to associate with people below our own expectations, do not dream of surrounding yourself with more successful people; who in turn can contribute to our own success.

When I want to acquire a particular ability or habit or characteristic, I hang around with folks who already have the habit or characteristic, or with others who also want to develop it. What I see my associates doing has a profound effect on what I do.

If a 30-second commercial can sell us a product, doesn't it stand to reason that the people we choose to spend time with can sell us a lifestyle? Doesn't it also stand to reason that the type of shows we watch on TV or the type of music we listen to can influence our values?

Remember the mythical three monkeys? One monkey has his eyes covered, the second his ears, the third his mouth. Below the monkey figurines are signs that read: see no evil, hear no evil, and speak no evil. Those monkeys were geniuses!

Life is fun, but it's also serious. There are no practice runs. There are no directors running around saying "Take 2" or "Take 3." No! You get one shot and that's it. Since my choices are so powerful, I quit wasting my time hanging around negative folks who influence me to make bad choices.

That's my choice. I began developing this attitude one afternoon. I had just completed my third trip around the block. My roommate John was sitting on the front porch. "Why do you do all that walking?" John asked. He was middle age. He had been a Jesuit priest many years, until he lost the vision that inspired his vocation.

I plopped in a chair beside him. "What a stupid question," I said.

"Maybe it is, but the answer doesn't have to be stupid."

I looked at him. "What do you mean?"

"Think about the question. 'Why do you walk so much?'"

"So someday I can walk without this stupid cane."

"Do you see yourself walking without a cane?"

"Of course!"

"Then you probably will. We become the way we see ourselves."

I sighed and shrugged. Sometimes John got too heavy.

"Why are you talking like some kind of guru?"

John ignored my sarcasm. "Do you see yourself becoming like one of those winos you were hanging around last night?"

"No way!"

"Why do you hang around them?"

"Nothing better to do."

"I used to work in a mission. A lot of the folks who asked for help were going through some kind of personal tragedy, but many came because their parents had gone to missions and their friends went to missions and other places where they could get free handouts."

I look him in the eye. "Why'd you tell me that?"

"Why do you think I told you?"

I didn't say anything. Finally, "You told me because you think I'm gonna become like those winos I sometimes spend time talking with. But I'm not. I just enjoy talking with them. They've got some amazing stories."

John smiled and looked like he was remembering something. "Don't believe everything you hear. I don't know what you'll become. I was just saying." His aluminum lawn chair creaked as he got up and went inside.

I didn't immediately change the company I kept. I couldn't. Spending time with other folks who seemed to be beaten by life helped me to feel better about my own situation. But as I learned to accept my situation and my attitude toward life improved, I became more conscious of the type of folks I hung with.

What John said did get me to thinking about the type of people I wanted to influence me. As I thought, my choice of who I kept company with gradually changed.

Good advice as well as wisdom can come from unexpected sources, so I try to keep my mouth shut and consider all the input I hear before I say anything or discard any of it.

There is a psychological phenomenon that occurs within groups of like people (winos, entrepreneurs, whatever) have the desire for harmony in a decision-making group and overrides a realistic appraisal of alternatives. Huh? So this means that if the majority of the associates I spend time with do not have the values or goals I have and desire, this can wreak havoc on my fledgling desire to build relationships with individuals who have similar values, goals or thought processes that are prerequisites for business success.

"Creativity is so delicate a flower that praise tends to make it bloom while discouragement often nips it in the bud," said Alex Osborne, an advertising executive and the author of the creativity technique named "brainstorming".

"Like it or not, human creativity has increasingly become a group process. 'Many of us can work much better creatively when teamed up,'" said Osborne.

Therefore the implication of negative group influencers can sabotage us, our creativity and our business. The effects of these groups often include rationalization, peer pressure and complacency, contributing to fatal flaws when it comes to decision making.

Your conformity to group values and ethics that hinder your personal development will negatively impact your business and your life.

For both personal and business reasons, we do need to be aware of the company we keep. Negativity can be, and far too often is, *contagious!* Be mindful of this as it can have a more far-reaching influence on your life than most of us are aware of. Do what you can to surround yourself with positive, upbeat, helpful, and hopeful people. I think you will find this quite beneficial in maintaining your positive attitude, too.

Some individuals are very sensitive to an atmosphere of negativity. If you happen to be one of these people, monitor your mood when you are in the company of negativity or around negative people. I'm sure that for most of us, this negative attitude has an uncanny knack to bring you down as well. It's almost as if there is a virus going around that we can catch that doesn't have an injection for to make you immune to its influence. You can literally *pickup* this *bug* and your mood will then suffer, too. All in accordance with the company you keep!

We are far more capable of dealing with life's challenges if we do our best to maintain a positive attitude. We need to be mindful of negativity within our circle of friends and associates, not only in ourselves, but in our work environment, in our social lives, and even in our homes. Be aware of the *contagion* of negativity and of its presence in *the company we keep*! Change the company you keep so it's conducive to becoming the positive person you want to be.

CHAPTER 21

Turning Negative to Positive

Better to light a candle than to curse the darkness.
—Chinese Proverb

EVERYONE'S LIFE IS FILLED WITH NEGATIVES AND POSITIVES. We deal with them every day. The best way I have found to deal with negatives is to convert them to positives. In other words, take the glass *half empty* and see it as *half full*. Some people have this tendency by birth, but for some it has to be cultivated.

Practicing positive thinking is easy for some, but it's difficult for someone with chronic negative thoughts, someone close to losing hope. Sometimes, life is filled with so many challenges that we feel hopeless, and negativity rules. For at least 10 years after my motorcycle crash, negativity was fully in charge of my life.

Our mind is like a *tape* which repeats the events of our past. Positive thinking does not work for some because our tapes (our minds) keep repeating our failures. If we're unskilled at something, and we want to improve, we may not be able to improve until we erase our tape. We have to make up our minds to believe we can succeed (for example, Edit *your tape* with new info—out with the old, in with the new) for your positive thinking to work.

Before we can tackle a problem we must know its roots. Where does negative thinking come from? The list of places to be influenced with negative thoughts can start with the media, and include our workplace, our family, our significant-other, our government, our religion, any social institution and ourselves. We each have unique experiences in these categories. For me, my family and my faith have always been a positive influence. My most negative influencer has been myself.

Having negative thoughts play out like a movie that can only bring you pain, something that I've experienced many times throughout my life. Negative thoughts drain us of energy and keep us from being in the present moment. The more we give in to your negative thoughts, the stronger they become. I like the imagery of a small ball rolling along the ground, and as it rolls, it becomes bigger and faster.

That's what one small negative thought can turn into: a huge, speeding ball of ugliness. On the contrary, a small positive thought can have the same effect blossoming into a beautiful outcome.

Have you ever thought about the power of your thoughts? One thing I've learned since my injury is this: not only are negative thoughts destructive, they're also addictive. Luckily, the addiction to negative thinking can be treated like any other addiction.

To chase away the dark clouds of negativity, to turn my negative thoughts into positive ones, to change limits to possibilities, these eight ideas have worked for me. I offer them to you as a road map for happy travels.

Smile: I didn't do much of this for years. My friend John B. from Toastmasters got me back in the habit of smiling when nobody was around, just to understand how good it feels to smile. It helped! My mood improved and the stress I felt lessened. Since it takes fewer muscles to smile than to frown, I even conserved energy.

Surround yourself with positive people. To get myself out of downward spirals, I called a friend who I knew could give me constructive, loving feedback. I have a few friends who I know well enough to help me put things in perspective instead of feeding my negative thinking.

Change the tone of your thoughts from negative to positive. For example, instead of thinking, "We are going to have a hard time adjusting to our living situation," think, "We may face some challenges in our living situation, but we will come up with solutions that we'll both be happy with."

Don't be a victim. You create your life—be an instigator—take responsibility. The way I was thinking and acting, you would think I couldn't change anything. But I could and eventually did. The main thing I changed was my attitude. Changing my thinking from that of a victim, who's hopelessly stuck, to someone who's in control gradually changed my mood by giving me power to think like a winner.

1) Winners know it's not all about them.
2) Winners care about others.
3) Winners know how to love and be loved.
4) Winners treat others like they're also winners.
5) Winners know how to lose like a winner.
6) Winners live without regrets because they do their best.

Help someone. Take the focus away from you and do something nice for another person. My favorite person to help is Wayne. My paralyzed friend, who is stuck in a nursing home type facility, always cheers me when I see the cheer and courage of someone who's been dealt a very rough hand.

Remember that no one is perfect and let yourself move forward. It's easy for me to dwell on my mistakes, but making amends, in whatever form that may take, learning from my mistake and moving forward, without looking back, is the best way for me to deal with any problems I create.

Sing. I don't remember lyrics very well, but I love singing, and I do remember a couple lyrics. One of the coolest feelings I ever had is when my best friend Bonnie was experiencing a rare moment of discouragement and I lifted her spirits by having her sit on the couch beside me as I sang her a song.

List five things that you are grateful for right now. Being grateful helps me appreciate what I already have. Here's my list: Friends, a healthy family (my mom's biopsy came back clean), being cancer free, my Winners Don't Quit Association business, and clear mind.

Read positive quotes. I like to place Post-It notes with positive quotes on my computer, fridge door, and mirror as reminders to stay positive. Also, I'd like to share with you a quote by an unknown author that was shared in a meditation class that I attended:

> Watch your thoughts, they become words.
> Watch your words, they become actions.
> Watch your actions, they become habits.
> Watch your habits, they become your character.
> Watch your character, it becomes your destiny.
> Happy positive thinking!

Following these eight ideas helped me change my negative thoughts to positive ones. But I'm only human and humans love to hold onto their addictions. If you want to rid your mind of negative thoughts and a negative thought pops into your head, pop it back out by thinking of something positive.

The more positive sayings you know and the more positive books you read, the easier it will be to replace that negative thought with something positive. Although Seattle drivers seem to manage it, most people's minds are never completely empty. I'm just kidding. If it wasn't for Seattle drivers, I probably wouldn't have gotten my license back. Luckily, being brain damaged fits me right into Seattle traffic.

Anyway, at least one thought is always on our minds. Because our minds cannot maintain a vacuum, we can't replace a negative thought with nothing. And it doesn't help to replace one negative thought with another negative thought. We need a positive thought to replace the negative thought.

The more positive thoughts and memories we store up from inspirational bios on the Internet, books, songs or friends, the easier it will be to let go of the negative and welcome the positive. And when we celebrate our abilities, we'll begin discovering possibilities in situations where we used to find limitations. Remember, there are NO LIMITS, except those we create for ourselves.

Our minds are like pharmacies where we can pick up prescriptions for either positive or negative thoughts. Our relationships and our circumstances demonstrate which type of prescription we most often pick up.

In today's demanding world, it is very easy to succumb to the negative ways of life. Negative thinking is a habit, and some of us don't even know we do it. Turning our mind from negative to positive thinking mode is something everyone can achieve. And the wonderful thing is that positive thinking takes the same amount of energy as negative thinking.

Our illness is the negativity within us. We can turn negative energy into positive energy. Our persona becomes the positivity within us. Positive attitudes control everything; turning negatives into positives is our greatest power to impact our reality. Being positive does not mean ignoring the negative. *Being positive means overcoming the negative.*

CHAPTER 22

Changing our Minds

Your living is determined not so much by what life brings
To you as by the attitude you bring to life;
Not so much by what happens to you
As by the way your mind looks at what happens.

—Khalil Gibran

We are shaped by our thoughts; we become what we think.
When the mind is pure, joy follows like a shadow that never leaves.

—Buddha

I HAVE SPENT MANY YEARS working on my health and happiness. I learned early on how my thoughts and my mind affect every experience I have. I began reading and learning about the health of my mind and how I could use my mind to benefit my life and my overall happiness. An early observation was that there are enough obstacles out there in our big, wide, wonderful world. The last thing I need to do is sabotage my dreams from within.

There are several different factors that affect health and happiness including nutrition, lifestyle, exercise, stress, family and career. However the one big factor that in my experience often gets overlooked is the health of the mind. It seemed to me that in order to create and maintain a healthy and happy life the work must begin with the mind.

Our thoughts are extremely powerful and can control all aspects of our life including our health. I believe that the majority of people out in this big world are only partially aware of the thoughts that go through their head.

Immediately after my motorcycle crash, I was only vaguely aware of all the jumble of thoughts that passed through my head. I wasn't even remotely aware of how those thoughts were affecting my reality and my feelings. To actually focus and be aware of each and every thought form that you think can be exhausting.

Thoughts can become habitual and many people have been conditioned from a very early age to have negative thought patterns. Those negative thought patterns get stuck within the subconscious mind and can literally shape who you are and how you react to your environment. Because of my poor self-esteem after my motorcycle crash, I had some real work to do.

The good news is that habits are meant to be broken and it was possible for me to take control of my thoughts again and make them work for me as opposed to working against me. I clearly remember thinking "Oh boy, I have some major work to do here!"

With that realization began my journey in taking the proper steps to create a healthy mind with the hopes of creating a far healthier and happier life.

Progress Not Perfection: Overcoming our darkest tragedies and endure our personal life traumas, we need to plant seeds for our own unique garden of resiliency, as I have done and many others have also done. There is a new life, a new beginning. We just have to wake up and live it. We can die striving for perfection, but we can live having progress. Focus on making progress and we'll reach excellence. Focus on always striving to be better than you were yesterday & you will reach new heights not only physically, but mentally and emotionally. You will experience an abundance of personal growth and become a better you.

Whether we are trying to achieve something or are recovering from something, the key to remember is: *Progress not Perfection.* Being dedicated to making progress implies that recovery of any kind is a process, which of course it is. "Progress, not perfection" is a quote I love and that has helped me through all kinds of situations, including rehab.

Too many times I have focused on the end result. Too many times I thought I was failing because I wanted to be like someone else. I wanted to perform like someone else. (Comparing our insides to someone else's outsides is never a good idea.) Too many times I felt like stopping either because I was not measuring up to someone or because I was having challenges with the goals I had made.

When I learned to claim *progress instead of perfection*, I became able to move peacefully forward. I still get impatient, but it isn't so bad since I quit comparing myself to other people. I can be happy knowing that I am doing the best I can. Life does not have to be perfect to be wonderful.

Toastmasters: One great example of *progress, not perfection* is my life in Toastmasters. I attend meetings because I want to improve my communication and interaction skills. It's a long term process. Sure, I would love to have the skills of somebody else that I admire. But that's not the point. I have my own talents and skills, and the most important thing for me to remember is that I am making progress. It's really a great feeling to see progress. Yes, I'd love to have excellent eye contact, vocal variety, body movement and other skills. But I am happy to see improvement in these areas. I am happy to see results from the changes that I try. And that's what keeps me going. I don't get discouraged.

Effects of Brain Damage: Having lived with significant brain damage for three decades, I've learned that negative ideas, fostered in the mind of a person already facing challenges, will likely grow and flourish. It is important to remember that our minds are like fields of the most fertile soil. Just as soil can produce weeds or flowers, so the things we plant in our minds will grow and produce the results we have planted.

Luckily, this works both ways. The fertile soil of our minds grows anything we plant in it. Knowing this, why not make an effort to only concentrate on positive thoughts of peace and goodwill?

I don't think you know how strong you are until a tragedy hits you. Everything before reality hits is theory. Reality gives the opportunity to find out if we're strong enough to handle it or if we're one of those people who curl up and let nature take its course.

We are In Control of What We Think: Imagine you're in a theater. The curtain is about to go up on a play you directed and starred in. Will you be inspired, will you be moved to tears? Will you see things you admire or things you regret? Will there be some of both? The protagonist you create is of ultimate importance. The protagonist is you. In this theater of our minds, you are not only the producer, the director, actor or actress; you are the audience who will react to the play with either pride or shame.

I usually react with a combination of both pride and regret. We are in control of the movie. We decide the story line played out on stage. Will your story be one of someone who got a bad break or will it be the story of someone who overcame difficulties and did what was necessary to live a happy and productive life?

Keep Trying: Regrettable as they are, mistakes are part of human nature. It's impossible to live without ever making a mistake. Mistakes are in our genetics, they're in our psychological make-up. Depending on whether you're brain damaged or not and on how high you set the bar, we are destined to make a certain number of mistakes.

The key to living a happy and productive life is not to try to avoid every mistake, but to keep trying despite our mistakes. The more mistakes we make, the more successes we're likely to have.

It's like a salesperson. The more doors they knock on, the more times they'll fail to make a sale, but the more sales they're likely to make. In other words, the more mistakes I make the more successes it's possible to have.

A healthy mind will help you find your way through life, from birth through childhood, through teenage years, adulthood and into older age. Below are some well recognized activities to help in developing and keeping a *healthy mind.*

Being Active: Exercising makes us feel good and can help our mental health. It will also help us sleep better, and get the rest we need. Be active, get sweaty and feel great! Working out' doesn't have to be at the gym. Just BE ACTIVE and find something you love to do and start doing it. There are no good excuses to not live the healthiest life possible. Do a little each day, your body will thank you for it.

Lower Alcohol Intake: Over-use of alcohol can increase feelings of depression. Try not to dwell on past mistakes or negative things that have happened to you. We all make mistakes and stewing on things or worrying to excess will not change anything. Learn from the experience and move on. Addiction begins with the hope that something 'out there' can instantly fill up the emptiness inside. At first, addiction starts as a pleasure, but the intensity of this pleasure gradually diminishes and the addiction is then maintained to avoid feeling uncomfortable.

Be with People Who Make Us Happy-and make the people we are with happy. Connecting with friends and family is key. Keep communicating and interacting, and tell those we trust how we are feeling if we're going through tough times. Talking to others and seeking help early can be very helpful in reducing depression, anxiety and distress. Never apologize for being sensitive or emotional. Let this be a sign that you've got a big heart and aren't afraid to let others see it. Showing your emotions is a sign of strength.

Keep Learning: To keep our minds both healthy and active, we must continue to learn. What we learn becomes a part of who we are. Aristotle said, "Educating the heart, without educating the mind, is no education at all." By learning a new sport, language, or to learn to play an instrument will all contribute to the process of exercising our minds. "Education is not the learning of facts, but the training of the mind to think."-Albert Einstein. By reading books, we are taking an active interest in feeding our brain with positive information. If we are not willing to learn, no one can help us. If we are determined to learn, no one can stop us. The capacity to learn is a gift. The ability to learn is a skill. The willingness to learn is a choice.

Keep A Positive Attitude: A positive attitude gives us power over our circumstances, instead of our circumstances having power over us. Having a positive attitude can provide a sense of well-being and be helpful especially when we are going through tough times. If we can develop a positive outlook on the way we see and do things it can lead to a greater sense of well-being. Well-being can mean different things to different people but some common features include having a sense of purpose, feeling good and functioning well, having control in your life and the options to change things if necessary, as well as achieving goals you set for yourself.

When free of depression, anxiety, addictions, excessive stress and worry and other psychological problems, we are more able to live our lives to the fullest. Peace of mind is a natural condition and is available to everyone.

Good mental health strengthens and supports our ability to have healthy relationships, make good life choices, maintain physical health and well-being, handle natural ups and downs of life and discover and grow to our potential!

Running away from your problems is a race you'll never win. Although none of us can go back and make a new start, we all can start from now and make a brand new end. Accept no one's definition of your life; define yourself!

"Yesterday I was clever so I wanted to change the world. Today I am wise so I am changing myself." –Rumi.

CHAPTER 23

Cancer–How Bad Is It?

Cancer is messy and scary.
You throw everything at it, but don't forget to throw love at it.
It turns out that love might be the best weapon of all.
—Regina Brett
The friend in my adversity I shall always cherish most.
I can better trust those who helped to relieve the gloom of my dark hours
than those who are so ready to enjoy with me the sunshine of my
prosperity.
—Ulysses S. Grant

THE "C" WORD FILLS MOST PEOPLE WITH DREAD. According to a recent survey, the majority of people asked said that getting cancer was their number one fear. So it's understandable that my receiving a diagnosis of cancer was very daunting. When people hear they have cancer, they think the worst really. Cancer has such scary connotations. But most people want to say 'OK, I've got cancer' and immediately get out of the doctor's office, run home and take in what's happening. When I got home, it was time to think about the information I'd received. Once my shock subsided, there was a flood of emotions to deal with. I wondered if this cancer diagnosis was a death sentence. They say that's normal. It takes a while to absorb the information and come to terms with the situation

When you're first diagnosed with cancer, you can have so many questions that it can be overwhelming. How will it affect my family? How will I cope with the treatment? How will I cope with losing a body part? Am I going to die? It's like Kareem Abdul-Jabbar said, "When the doctor told me I had cancer, I was scared."

There are many unknowns, and it's natural to feel that you've lost some control over your life. Being able to answer these questions will help you cope and regain that sense of control.

It can be hard in such a difficult situation, but trying to be positive can really help you to cope. Try focusing on the positive things that you do know, and avoid negative thoughts that may not be true.

Try to encourage yourself whenever possible, and be proud of your strength and courage. Remember to enjoy the times that you're feeling well, and have fun with your family and friends. "The love of family and the admiration of friends is much more important than wealth and privilege."--Charles Kuralt.

Accepting my circumstances required me to do at least two things. The first is to make the most of the abilities that I still have, in fact, to celebrate them, which included hobbling along with my cane and exercising. The second key for me was to accept my situation was learning what I call my "ABCs."

> **A:** Accept the Book I've Been Given.
>
> **B:** Believe I Can Write a Happy Ending.
>
> **C:** Care About Myself by Caring About others.

There's a fear that goes through you when you are told you have cancer. It's so hard in the beginning to think about anything but your diagnosis. It's the first thing you think about every morning. Gilda Radner said "Having cancer gave me membership in an elite club I'd rather not belong to."

Often, people who have had a cancer experience stand back and reflect on their lives, perhaps make new friends, change their lifestyle, and embrace life more. It is astonishing how life altering, or life changing, events do to deepen our thinking and give us a whole new perspective on life. Suddenly our significance, or lack of significance, becomes quite clear. In the following ABC formula, I use the word "book" to represent life:

A: Accept the Book I've Been Given: It's not up to us if we're given a leather-bound, gold-embossed hardback or a cheaply-glued paperback, but what the pages say is up to us. What do your pages say?

B: Believe I Can Write a Happy Ending: For me, having a divine source, makes it easier to believe I can write a happy ending to my life book. And it makes it easier to believe in my capabilities and my possibilities. Believing in all that makes it easier to lighten up. After spending years being suicidal, depressed and afraid of my future, being able to lighten up and believe everything will work out is proof to me that believing in a divine source beats the alternative.

C: Care About Myself by Caring About others: The more I do for others, the better I feel about myself. And the better I feel about myself, the better I feel about others and life in general. Jennifer Aniston said "Cancer affects all of us, whether you're a daughter, mother, sister, friend, coworker, doctor, and patient."

Cancer is a serious malady. I've known people who waged painful battles against it for years only to finally die from it. In no way am I minimizing the suffering other people have had to endure. National cancer campaigner Elizabeth Edwards said before she died, "In a sense, having cancer takes you by the shoulders and shakes you."

Often people who have battled cancer find new meaning in life, and recognize how precious the time we have is. They get out of bad relationships and into good ones; they stop dreaming of possibilities and they start making them come true; they take risks, enjoy new adventures, and set purpose-driven goals that are truly remarkable. And in the end, they inspire others in a ripple effect that goes beyond one's wildest imagination.

Over 30 years after my crash, my best friend Bonnie and I went to one last doctor appointment, this time with an anesthesiologist, before my cancer operation the next week.

Before the operation, my primary care physician told me that dealing with the cancer would not be easy. Obviously I wasn't prepared for my motorcycle crash. Hearing my cancer diagnosis was a completely different set of circumstances. After researching and understanding my choices and circumstances, I felt I had the life skills to cope with my diagnosis of cancer. The operation went as well as it could have.

The cancer I endured was minor compared to many types of cancer. In fact, compared to my head injury and partial paralysis, my cancer operation and recovery was an afternoon walk in the park.

Friendships can have a major impact on your health and well-being. Good friends are good for your health. . Friends can help you celebrate good times and provide support during bad times.

Many adults find it hard to develop new friendships or keep up existing friendships. Friendships may take a back seat to other priorities, such as work or caring for children or aging parents. You and your friends may have grown apart due to changes in your lives or interests. Or maybe you've moved to a new community and haven't yet found a way to meet people.

Developing and maintaining good friendships takes effort. The enjoyment and comfort friendship can provide, however, makes the investment worthwhile. I can attest that having friends is what pulled me through the emotional challenges of having cancer. The philosopher Aristotle said, "In poverty and other misfortunes of life, true friends are a sure refuge.

My best friend Bonnie was priceless during the seven months of preparation before my operation and the following six months after the surgery. Genuine friends are not only priceless; they are essential to our survival and an important part of survival preparedness. Genuine friends listen thoughtfully to our sorrows, laugh with us and celebrate our joy and victories as though they were their own. True friendship is far more than regular association and cordial behavior. Once friendship is established, the status of poverty, wealth, honest human failings or distance cannot sever the bonds of true affection and mutual support. I call her name and there she was ready to do research, take me to my doctor's appointments, coordinate after-care and most importantly, I knew she was in my court, on my team throughout the entire process.

Quality counts more than quantity. While it's good to cultivate a diverse network of friends and acquaintances, you also want to nurture a few truly close friends who will be there for you through thick and thin. And Bonnie has been by my side assisting me with many parts of my life. A close friend is a mirror of your own self, someone with whom you realize that, though autonomous, you are not alone.

When she first saw me doing a 2009 New Year's Eve comedy show at a casino, for the final hour before midnight, Bonnie couldn't have known the mutual stresses and the mutual joys we would eventually share. I concluded that comedy show with the serious message of "Let's go into the New Year accepting and focusing on what we have instead of worrying about what we don't have."

Being the Executive Director for an EMS and Trauma Care Council, Bonnie happened to be looking for specialized entertainment for an upcoming retreat for approximately 100 fire departments, 10 major hospitals and a vast collection of paramedics, doctors, nurses and other emergency room workers.

Seeing me, a half-paralyzed motorcycle crash survivor and veteran of trauma care with a contagious sense of humor and some poignant observations, gave Bonnie a great idea of how well her people would be able to relate to my humor and my positive message. With her organizational skills and my small but sincere contribution of insightful humor, the retreat proved a smashing success. Bonnie and I have continued growing closer ever since.

What a joy Bonnie has added to my life ever since that day nearly five years ago, and what a comfort it was to have her as my best friend when I was told I had cancer. Just as the medical community advises, I had my PSA checked shortly after turning 50.

As we prepared for my upcoming battle with cancer, I was filled with relief that I had a best friend like Bonnie helping me. Being a wonderful patient advocate, Bonnie spent hours researching my cancer and treatment options and went with me to every doctor's appointment. She asked many pertinent questions so I would have all the information I needed to choose the best treatment option.

Life is hard as it is. There are too many rough roads to travel--too many chains to untangle. But no matter how cruel the world may be, life becomes less difficult when you have a good friend.

The only thing that is close to being as nice as having a best friend like Bonnie is being a best friend to someone like Bonnie. Being a good friend isn't always easy, but taking the time to nurture a lasting friendship is worth every ounce of effort. As the years pass, some people will stay by your side, but many won't, and you'll realize that each friendship you keep is priceless. Of course, to have a good friend, you must be one, and it takes a lot of effort and care. To be a good friend, you have to establish trust by being there for your friend when you're needed, during both hard and easy times.

CHAPTER 24

Conquering Cancer with Friends

Marian Bryant, herself a cancer survivor,
offers this message of hope and love:
Cancer is so limited... It cannot cripple love.
It cannot shatter hope. It cannot corrode faith.
It cannot eat away peace. It cannot destroy confidence.
It cannot kill friendship. It cannot shut out memories.
It cannot silence courage. It cannot reduce eternal life.
It cannot quench the Spirit.
—Marian Bryant

"I get by with a little help from my friends,"
— Paul McCartney

IN GOOD TIMES, and especially when life sends us challenges, having friends is a never ending source of courage and joy. This is when the kindness and generosity of our friends truly matter.

At 11:30 that evening, Bonnie and I were finally led from an intensive care recovery room outside the Surgery Pavilion to a nice corner room of the UW Medical Center patient tower area. Somebody rolled in a "cot" for Bonnie that was more like a bed. It came with a mattress, blankets and pillows, all the necessary comforts for a well-earned rest. It had been an emotional day of waiting through surgery and intensive care that started with arriving at the hospital at 5:30 in the morning. Actually, the anticipation had started several weeks before.

I was relieved to have come out of the surgery with a positive report from the surgeon. At this point, we both felt very grateful for the positive experiences and the professional treatment and care by physicians, nurses and staff at the University of Washington Medical Center.

My being in a jovial mood put Bonnie at ease and she pulled out her phone to take pictures. Her first photo is of me and my swollen face, but that isn't enough. She starts taking pictures of different young pretty nurses posing with me. I'd be fibbing if I didn't admit that I thoroughly enjoyed all of the attention. And I milked it.

I believe I have a great sense of humor, and I used it generously being greatly relieved to be healthy again. In fact, I felt even giddy and light-hearted to know all had gone as well as anyone could have hoped for. Everybody was laughing and joking and sharing in my joy at learning of a positive outcome.

The humor was infectious. The sound of the on-going laughter from my room was far more contagious than any cough, sniffle, or sneeze. Laughter triggers healthy physical changes in the body. Humor and laughter strengthen your immune system, boosts your energy, diminishes pain, and protects you from the damaging effects of stress. Best of all, this priceless medicine was right up my alley, fun, free, and easy to share.

Nurse Enoch, a young man from Uganda, was one of many nurses in and out of my room. I am extremely happy to make this young man's acquaintance and look forward to a long-lasting friendship. When laughter is shared, it binds people together and increases happiness and intimacy.

Look for the humor in a bad situation, and uncover the irony and absurdity of life. This will help improve your mood and the mood of those around you. Not long after my release from the hospital, a pathology report declared that I am 100% cancer free. Halleluiah! Life was coming back to normal again!

Cancer Brought Out Our Best: All the positive attention had me feeling like a celebrity and *almost* wishing I could afford more cancer surgeries. Although this first, and hopefully last, cancer operation went way better than the doctors' careful prediction, the life-changing results of cancer were not lost on me. I happen to have been very fortunate. I am also thankful for the lessons I have learned from this particular event in my life and I am grateful for the positive outcome.

Upon heading home the day after my surgery, I was feeling sore and tired, but very thankful. I'm not only thankful for Bonnie, I'm grateful for the friends I know will be visiting me during my recovery. During this time, I discovered the *sweet little things* that made my friends a dearer part of my life.

Thank you Pastor Gary. You're the best. Seeing your warm and bright smile, shining like the beam from a lighthouse, the morning of the surgery and the day after surgery, made me realize that my support group was much larger than just my immediate family. Pastor Gary is continually on-call to provide wisdom, spiritual guidance and emotional support. I felt so grateful to have the support of the church I attend. Even if the God of my understanding didn't include church, I would still want the positive relationships I've developed there.

Neither of us slept much, if at all, in the hospital. Hospital leadership knows patients need to sleep — for emotional health, for wound healing, to maintain a strong immune system — and yet the drama of fractured and broken sleep played out that night. My vital signs needed to be taken every four hours to make sure I was stable. My nurses came into my room in the middle of the night, scanned my wristband and signed on to the computer in the room before they left. Hospital nursing staff started "morning labs" at 4 a.m.

I was told that they try to bundle nighttime patient care, so they disturb the patient only once, but it's not always possible. Most of the nurses were very quiet, but I startled easily and couldn't get back to sleep.

Bonnie and I laid pretty low the first couple of days following my surgery. Any surgery will leave you feeling tired. Your body is healing. Bonnie and I finally closed our eyes and got some much needed sleep.

On my second or third day home, still too weak to sit up for very long, I sat at my computer desk. I felt a need to be creative, but my computer wouldn't boot up! Huh? *I don't have the time or the energy for this.* Luckily, my brother had worked in Boeing technical support until later moving to a different branch, but his computer technology skills were still very proficient.

I picked up my cell phone. "Hi Harvey, do you have a minute?"

Within a few minutes, after some complex instructions I wouldn't have figured out, I'm happily creating an earlier chapter of this story on my smooth-running computer. Knowing a computer genius is cool. Having a computer genius for a friend and a brother is beyond cool.

Bonnie had cleared her calendar so she was free to stay with me during the first days following my surgery, but she had other responsibilities. She couldn't just stay with me on even a semi-permanent basis. I knew the day when she had to leave would come, and I was ready.

Thanks to the principles that rehabilitation has taught me about getting along with others and building mutually beneficial friendships, I called a friend from church. I've been friends with Phil for way over a decade. He knew about my cancer operation and was quick to say he'd be over right after work.

"What do you want me bring for dinner?" he asked.

"Thanks for your incredible friendship, Phil. Don't worry about bringing anything," I said. "Linda Jean is bringing chicken, mashed potatoes and coleslaw, and a dessert." Friends pick us up when we fall down, and if they can't pick us up, they lie down and listen for a while.

The cool thing about the chicken dish is that she put in toy plastic snakes to correlate with a missionary who shared his experiences with Singly Focused about a mission trip he took to Viet Nam, where snakes were a common part of the menu.

So it went for the next several days. I had more food than ever and it was brought by smiling friends from the singles group at church.

My parents stopped in to see how I was doing. They knew about my surgery. They've both had cancer and helped Bonnie and I choose a treatment option. Being older, they had opted to treat their cancer with radiation. Seeing them was great. I only wish I'd invited them to stay and watch the video someone brought.

Cancer Helps Me Man Up: That evening's entertainment with Phil resulted in my having a new all-time favorite movie. "The Count of Monte Cristo" has such a complex and cleverly written story line that I will never forget it.

As we watched, I suddenly grabbed the remote and pressed the pause button. I absolutely had to write down part of what the Count said as he saved an awkward situation at an important dinner party with a brilliant toast.

"Life is a storm," he said to a nervous then pleased and confident young man.

"You will bask in the sunlight one moment; be shattered on the rocks the next. What makes you a man is what you do when that storm comes. You must look into that storm and shout:
'Do your worst for I will do mine!'"

Just think, if I had not come down with cancer, I may have never seen that classic movie or heard and been able to pass on that incredible quotation. Again, my long-time friendship with Phil has had many blessings over the years.

It was February 6, less than a week after my surgery, and the Green Bay Packers played the Pittsburgh Steelers (I love both teams) for a Super Bowl game at the Cowboys stadium in Arlington, Texas. Packers won that day. Thanks also for the Super Bowl munchies Cheryl and Lori. A Super Bowl party with pizza, chicken wings and nachos is pretty tasty! Thank you my sweet friends. True friends intentionally step outside of their own world to sincerely ask and find out what's going on in someone else's life.

I love happy endings. Since we are all authors of our own life books, it is not surprising that I want to write a happy ending to my life book. The relationships that pass through our lives are fundamental in determining how happy our books turn out.

Because of the scientific medical advances and new methods for treating cancer and because of the many friends who banded around me during my time of need, I feel appreciative and thankful. True friendship isn't about being there when it's convenient, it's about being there when it's not.

My cancer experience reminded me of past tough life lessons after my motor cycle crash. This time dealing with a major health issue proved to be a much more pleasant experience, for which I am most grateful. As I have grown up, I have realized it becomes less important to have a ton of friends, and more important to have real ones.

CHAPTER 25

Expecting Success

You always pass failure on the way to success.
—Mickey Rooney

I don't measure a man's success by how high he climbs
but how high he bounces when he hits bottom.
—George S. Patton

THE NUMBER ONE REASON why people are unsuccessful or unhappy is because they do not know what they want out of life. You see, life is a like a blank canvas. It is up to each individual to pick the colors they wish to paint and draw any picture they please. If a person does not choose to pick their colors or picture to paint, they can be certain that someone else who does know what they want will pick it for them.

Success is a journey, not a destination. The doing is often more important than the outcome. When going into any situation, whether it is as simple as a phone call, or as complex as a lifetime, knowing what you want is essential to getting what you want. It is the destination which we must have in mind clearly prior to starting any journey.

How we approach opportunities, obstacles, etc. in our lives is determined more by our attitudes than by the material resources we have or don't have. In my experience, I've seen people fail and people succeed. For the most part, the people who succeed are the people willing to put their whole heart into their attempt because they believe they can achieve their goal. People I've seen who seem to approach things with the expectation of failing, getting turned down, being rejected, etc. usually do. They might not think they do, but if they were honest about their approach, far more step in expecting a defeat than a win. Maybe it's self-doubt. Maybe it's being rejected in the past. Maybe it's not feeling worthy. Whatever the reason, it's sad and it's keeping many from living their dream.

Our minds try to complete whatever we imagine, so if we see ourselves succeeding, chances are better that we will. Seneca said, "Wisdom does not show itself so much in precept as in life - in firmness of mind and a mastery of appetite. It teaches us to do as well as to talk; and to make our words and actions all of a color."

If our thoughts, talk, actions and being are all in sync, then we will be displaying wisdom and we will advance more rapidly and happily towards our goal. I think true stress comes from being out of line…where our actions are different from our thoughts and desires.

If we are walking in line with our thoughts and dreams, then there is no need to be stressed. I have learned that if we take care of our health, our minds, our spirit and we be who we are meant to be and seek love and happiness, we will have true success. Albert Einstein said that *"Your imagination is your preview of life's coming attractions and imagination is more important than knowledge. For knowledge is limited to all we now know and understand, while imagination embraces the entire world, and all there ever will be to know and understand."*

Whatever We Imagine
By James Ingram

Don't be afraid, I can meet you halfway
We can't always know where the road ends up.
But with some luck I know we can go wherever we imagine.

Why should we wait? Later on may be too late.
'Cause where can we run, when you see there's half a chance
That we might really become whatever we imagine.

And I imagine you and me just taking shots at what we see.
And if we fall we'll shake away the dust and just outlast them all

You ought to see all your heroes in me.
But if we get wise, we can break the walls we make.
And you can see in my eyes whatever we imagine

And I imagine you and me just taking shots at what we see.
So let the walls go down and we can try it again.
'Cause nobody can stop us now...

Let's face it -- You are going to fail, multiple times. It's what you do with them that will predict if you'll be an overall success. If you embrace the failure, learn from it and move on, then was it really a failure? If you flounder and flop after each failure and get gun shy then it for sure was. But if you learn a better or a different way of doing something, how can that be called a failure?

Everyone has bad habits. Some more than others, but we all have them. The most surprising habits I've seen is the habit of expecting things to go wrong. If you always expect to fail then chances are good that failure will follow you. IF you or your idea gets shot down today, that's okay. That just means you need to rework it and try again later or maybe try it in a different way. Timing and approach matter. It's normal to fail now and again, but it's completely different to think you're always going to fail.

When we have serious doubts about whether something will work, it shows in our efforts. We don't try as hard. Simply expecting success doesn't guarantee its achievement. Action is essential. However, if we don't expect success, we'll limit the actions required to achieve it. Few people have achieved success while doubting they could do it. There is power within intent. We can't go into the game expecting to lose.

Our minds try to complete whatever we imagine, so seeing ourselves succeeding, and chances are better that we will. "Do not fear mistakes. You will know failure. Continue to reach out." Benjamin Franklin.

In an earlier chapter on spirituality, I shared the steps I use to help chase away negative thoughts, now I'll share three choices that keep them from returning.

1.   I choose to ask questions and not make assumptions.

When people do or say things to us or about us, we automatically assume we know what these people are thinking or intending. We don't. We can only learn the truth by asking questions and seeking clarification. It helps me to not make assumptions or take things personally.

The truth is: criticism usually reveals more about the criticizer than about the criticized.

If I forget this and assume I know what someone means, it's easy for me to take things personally and feel angry and sorry for myself. "They don't like me, or they're out to get me," and other thoughts like that can fill my head—all examples of negative thinking.

It's no coincidence that in the dictionary the word "assume" is spelled: ASS-U-ME. In other words, assuming stuff makes an ass out of you and me, at least in the mind of the one doing the assuming. That's too perfect to be an accident.

For years my speech impairment made me feel so uncomfortable, I felt as if I was Froggy of the Little Rascals trying to fit into the Vienna Boys Choir. After I got out of the hospital, I began to assume that all "normal" people thought I was a mental case because of my speech impairment. This was particularly disturbing since I enjoy talking so much.

Keeping my mouth shut was the wrong option. By assuming I knew what people were thinking and that they were thinking derogatory things about me, I felt angry, depressed, and just plain miserable. Because I never asked what they were thinking, or if they were thinking about me at all, I'll never know if they even knew I was around.

It's entirely possible that all the negative emotions I was feeling were entirely of my own creation. One valuable lesson my journey taught me is to not assume that I know what other people think of me.

My rehabilitation process has taught me other useful lessons. For example, stumbling around the block while holding my cane off the ground, repeating words and phrases into a tape recorder, learning to tie my shoes with one hand, and holding my water till I reach the bathroom, all taught me the same lesson: success is closest when my hope for tomorrow's victory gets more attention than my memory of today's failure.

As I hobbled around the block holding my cane off the ground, my dream of one day walking without a cane kept me going. If my head had been full of memories of the time I fell and had to get several stitches in my eyebrow, I probably would have stayed sitting on the porch.

Having a poor memory can actually be a good thing. At least I had to buy only one CD. My memory used to be so bad that once I forgot I was paralyzed. I was walking normal—until someone reminded me I was paralyzed. "Oh yeah, thanks," I said, beginning to limp again.

Relearning to drive convinced me of another powerful choice. What you believe about yourself and your potential is more important than any limitations people say you have.

2. I don't take criticism personally.

Oscar Wilde once said about critics who wrote about his plays: "Criticism is a form of autobiography." He was right. Criticism reveals more about the critic than it does about the person or event being criticized. In his book *The Four Agreements,* Don Miguel Ruiz wrote, "Don't take anything personally." Nothing anyone ever says to you or does to you is about you. It is a projection of the feelings and reactions that are going on inside the person doing the criticizing.

Criticism used to bother me a great deal, even if I wasn't altogether sure it was directed at me. My self-esteem was so low that I automatically assumed that anything negative or derogatory was meant for me and was true. Two realizations helped me change how I perceived criticism.

(a) Even winners get criticized. But they can ignore it. They can evaluate its worth and discard what they don't believe has merit.

(b) Criticism is actually a gift. If someone gives you a gift and you refuse it, to whom does it belong? Just because someone criticizes me doesn't mean I have to even acknowledge it. But since it's free, it would be foolish if I didn't choose to at least examine it to see if it has any value.

It has taken me many years and hundreds of choices, some good and some not so good, to reach a level where I can again consider myself a winner. The key to being a winner is to not give up.

There are six characteristics that winners have.

Winners know it's not all about them.

Winners care about others.

Winners know how to love and be loved.

Winners treat others like they're also winners.

Winners know how to lose like a winner.

Winners do their best.

I fell a lot more times than I wanted to, but how many times I fell isn't what mattered. All that mattered is that I kept getting up. Life is like selling vacuum cleaners. The more doors you knock on, the more times you open yourself up to failure—but the more doors you knock on, the more sales you are going to make.

3. Whatever I do, I always do my best.

I want to live without any more regrets about what might have been if only I tried a little harder. Life is like a boxing match. Sometimes you're fighting someone who is stronger, faster, and smarter.

But you can still win. You've just gotta take his best shot and keep coming. As the American heavy-weight champion Jack Dempsey said, "A champion is someone who gets up when he can't." In other words, Winners Don't Quit!

Let me be very clear that I'm not talking about the Law of Attraction or wishful thinking. By expecting results you're setting yourself up for success. *Then* the massive action is started.

You must create a plan that supports your expectations. People can get a feel for your intentions. I once spoke with a friend prior to him going into a sales presentation. His words to me when I wished him luck was "don't get your hopes up, I probably won't get it." He was right.

Expectation is the root of all heartache. Of course it is. The very definition of heartache is when reality fails to live up to one's expectations. We don't often think of heartache that way, but there it is... Does that mean if I lower my expectations, I can avoid heartache? - Probably. Should I lower my expectations to avoid heartache? - Probably not.

Heartache beats expectation out of some people. They experience something so painful they're unwilling to expect very much out of love, work, family, friends, or anything else that gives life meaning. Expectation is risky. However, if expectation is the root of all heartache, then it's also the root of all joy, right?

Heartache happens when reality doesn't live up to expectation. Sometimes, reality meets or even exceeds expectation. So, while expectation is risky, it's also absolutely necessary for happiness. How can reality exceed our expectations if we don't have any?

The ones that find happiness are the ones that don't make excuses. If it's broke, they fix it. If it's wrong, they make it right.

WARNING: If you're making excuses *before* you begin something it's a sign that you are expecting to lose. Pay attention to how you think & feel about something. That great idea you have will never work if you have doubts about its success. You won't pour your blood, sweat, and tears into something unless you have the expectation you'll achieve your desired result. If it's important to you, you'll find a way. If it's not, you'll find an excuse to give up.

There are only two options, make progress, or make excuses.

The Victor

If you think you'll lose, you've lost,

for out in the world you'll find that…

Success begins with a person's will; it's all in the state of mind.

For many a game is lost before even a step is run.

And many a coward fails before his work is begun.

Think big and your deed will grow; think small and you will fall behind.

Think that you can and you will; It's all in the state of mind and belief.

If you think that you are out-classed, you are;

you've got to think high to rise.

You've got to be sure of yourself before you can win the prize.

Life's battles don't always go to the strongest or fastest man.

But sooner or later the person who wins

is the person who thinks he or she can.

classes: those who are immovable, those who are movable, and those who move!" He also said, "Do not fear mistakes. You will know failure. Continue to reach out."

You deserve success. You should expect it. And you should know you need to move and put some energy behind it. You can do it. I can do it. We can all do it, so just do it!

CHAPTER 26

Choosing Happiness

I'd always believed that a life of quality, enjoyment, and wisdom were my human birthright and would be automatically bestowed upon me as time passed. I never suspected that I would have to learn how to live – that there were specific disciplines and ways of seeing the world I had to master before I could awaken to a simple, happy, uncomplicated life.
—Dan Millman

With time and patience the mulberry leaf becomes a silk gown.
—Chinese Proverb

IN OUR NOT-TOO-DISTANT PAST, humans were mostly focused on survival. Worrying about things like whether you'd have something to eat when you were hungry or if something would eat you when it was hungry were more important than pondering the idea of happiness. And although there are still people around the world who struggle with meeting their basic needs, most of us have the luxury of a little free time. We often spend at least a portion of it wondering whether we're happy, and if not, what we need to make us happy.

Some people think that they'd be truly happy with themselves if they had a perfect body, a high-powered job, a lot of money or fame. However, there are plenty of well-known, well-off, attractive people who aren't happy. The opposite is also true. Dr. Robert Biswas-Diener, who works in the field of positive psychology, surveyed a group of

Maasai warriors in Kenya about their happiness. The Maasai don't generally have the things that people in the developed world consider to be happiness generators, such as material wealth. But they still overwhelmingly think of themselves as happy. This doesn't mean that wealthy people can't be happy -- it just means that being wealthy doesn't automatically confer happiness. The same goes for any other attribute.

So if happiness doesn't come from what you do or what you have, where does it come from? According to Dr. Robert Holden, founder of The Happiness Project, "those looking for happiness often don't realize they already have it". Being happy with yourself isn't so much about pursuing it, but finding things that you can do to help you recognize your happiness

When I am feeling happy and positive, I feel like there's nothing I can't do. Big deal! We all feel capable of conquering the world when things are going our way. But what about times when things aren't going our way? If you're like me, sometimes you feel depressed.

Happiness is not something we can buy. And it's not something others can give us. Can we learn to be happy? Happiness is about being connected. If we learn to be more deeply connected with others, we become happier. Notice how happiness increases when you practice loving-kindness. After all, happiness is not an individual matter.

Are you kind to yourself? Maybe you are a person who is kind to everyone, yet is still unhappy? If so, let me ask you: how do you treat yourself? Are you kind and loving? Do you forgive yourself for mistakes? Do you encourage yourself? No? There you have it then.

Loving-kindness makes us happier. Loving-kindness is a heartfelt wish for happiness and wellbeing. When we are loving and kind, we tend to be more patient, tender, gentle, and generous. You can see that loving-kindness is the perfect antidote to dislike, resentment, hatred, fear, and bitterness. And there is a clear connection between loving-kindness and happiness.

Participation in acts of kindness releases serotonin in our brains. Serotonin is a substance that has TREMENDOUS health benefits, including making us feel more blissful. Selflessly helping someone is a super powerful way to feel good inside. What's even cooler about this kindness kick is that not only will you feel better, but so will people watching the act of kindness. How extraordinary is that? A side note is that the job of most anti-depressants is to release more serotonin. Move over pharmaceutical companies, kindness is moving back into the neighborhood.

Winners have the ability to manufacture their own positive attitude. No matter what the situation, the successful diva is the chick who will always find a way to put a positive spin on it. She knows failure only as an opportunity to grow and learn a new lesson from life. People who think positively see the world as a place packed with endless opportunities.

The happiest people on the planet are the ones who have deep, meaningful relationships. Did you know studies show people's mortality rates doubled when they are lonely? WHOA! There's more than a warm fuzzy feeling that comes from having an active circle of good friends who you can share your experiences with. There's actually life!

Harboring feelings of hatred is horrible for your well-being. You see, your mind doesn't know the difference between past and present emotion. When you "hate" someone, and you're continuously thinking about it, those negative emotions are toxic for your well-being. You put yourself in a state of suckerism (technical term) and it stays with you throughout your day.

Deep happiness cannot exist without slowing down to enjoy the joy. It's easy in a world of wild stimuli and omnipresent movement to forget to embrace life's enjoyable experiences. When we neglect to appreciate, we rob the moment of its magic. It's the simple things in life that can be the most rewarding if we remember to fully experience them.

When I'm feeling depressed, I do two things. First, I pray for help. Everybody has his or her own way of connecting with their personal idea of a greater power, and that's as it should be. I think connecting with your own idea of God is where something strange and wonderful can happen. When we practice spirituality or religion, we recognize that life is bigger than us. We surrender the silly idea that we are the mightiest thing ever. It enables us to connect to the source of all creation and embrace a connectedness with everything that exists. Some of the happiest and most accomplished people I know feel that they're here doing work they're "called to do."

Having a personal spiritual relationship is what really matters. Having a personal relationship with someone else's idea of the divine didn't help me. Behavior and thought modification happens for me when I'm connected with my understanding of a power greater than and outside of myself.

Alcoholics Anonymous taught me how powerful it is to turn my life and my will over to the care of God *as I understand him.* I do not want to turn this line of thinking into a debate. I'm only saying that things seem to go much better when I trust the God of my understanding instead of trying to control things. For everyone who agrees, there's probably someone who disagrees. Oh well. Maybe if we had more accepting and trusting and less trying to control, we could all be happier.

Flow is a state in which it feels like time stands still. It's when you're so focused on what you're doing that you become one with the task. Action and awareness are merged. You're not hungry, sleepy, or emotional. You're just completely engaged in the activity that you're doing. Nothing is distracting you or competing for your focus.

The second thing I do when I'm feeling down is look around and see if I can find somebody to help. Most folks don't go around talking about their problems. But if I show genuine interest in someone's situation, it is amazing how willing people are to share with someone who is willing to help. It's kind of like I feel like I can conquer the world with one hand when you're holding the other.

The happiest people on the planet are the ones who have deep, meaningful relationships. Did you know studies show people's mortality rates doubled when they are lonely? WHOA! There's a warm fuzzy feeling that comes from having an active circle of good friends who you can share your experiences with. We feel connected and a part of something more meaningful than our lonesome existence unities, especially in trying times.

Years ago, before she died from heart problems, I had a real long term friend named Sharon who I learned a lot from. When she was at work and dealing with customers, she was happy and cheerful. But when stressed from working overtime, she had no problem telling someone exactly what she thought about something.

Being wholeheartedly dedicated to doing something comes fully-equipped with an ineffable force. Magical things start happening when we commit ourselves to doing whatever it takes to get somewhere. When you're fully committed to doing something, you have no choice but to do that thing. Counter-intuitively, having no option -- where you can't change your mind -- subconsciously makes humans happier because they know part of their purpose.

When we first met, she lived in the same condo complex I did. She was amazing. All by herself, with no help from the government or relatives, she not only raised her two kids to be responsible professional adults, she raised them to be happy, unselfish people.

How you respond to frustrating trials is what shapes your character. Sometimes crap happens -- it's inevitable. There's no clearer way to say it. Forrest Gump knows how to have a purpose and just do it.

Forrest Gump: "When I got tired, I slept. When I got hungry, I ate. When I had to go, you know, I went."

Elderly Southern Woman: "And so, you just ran?"

Forrest Gump: "Yeah."

It can be hard to come up with creative solutions in the moment manure is flying toward the fan. It helps to have healthy strategies for coping pre-rehearsed, on-call, in your arsenal and at your disposal.

What's even more amazing are the single parents all over the country who are motivated by love to do things for their children that would inspire anyone who really looked. The woman I mentioned earlier, who was one of the last polio victims and as a single parent raised five kids, became a comedian after becoming a single parent. She used her love, her determination and her comedy earnings to raise her kids without help from anyone.

When you appreciate what you have, the value of what you have appreciates. In other words, being grateful for the happiness you already have will bring you an even deeper sense of happiness.

And that's without having to go out and buy anything. It makes sense. We're gonna have a hard time ever being happy if we aren't thankful for what we already have.

When her kids were raised, she could finally slow down. In her free time, she found and married a man with whom she's very happy. I love true stories like these. To me, stories of people turning desperate situations into happy ones are springs of hope. When I hear a story of a person doing something ordinary people do not do, I feel empowered to do more than I thought I could.

Having been through years of rehab in Seattle's largest trauma center, I have seen dozens of situations that looked hopeless. I haven't kept track of everyone, so it's possible that some situations were hopeless. But I'm friends with a few former patients and I've seen their lives gradually and dramatically improve. I've seen firsthand how powerful the human spirit is.

My own situation seemed hopeless, but with patience and hard work, mostly patience, my situation has changed to one in which I'm free to be happy.

Being happy living with brain damage and physical impairments is an art that requires a specific set of realizations. I have now been living with disabilities longer than I lived without them. Learning to humbly accept that I can no longer do many of the things I once could, and learning to humbly accept that I may never learn many of the things I once could have learned are the two biggest lessons in humility I thought I would ever have to learn.

The former are ongoing lessons in humility. A new lesson in humility presented itself when my doctor told me I have cancer. Cancer! Why me? Why now? I don't have time for cancer I am finally building my speaking business to be helpful on an international level.

My deep faith has helped and my many teachers have helped me to get my message out to a lot of people who have told me they feel blessed and grateful. Would the God of my understanding allow me to get cancer? Sure. Why not? God, as I understand him, may not always prevent me from experiencing problems, but the understanding I have is that He will always give me what I need to get through the problem.

Looking back on my rehabilitation, I honestly thought that patience with my own situation is the most valuable lesson I've learned. But that's not true. Humility is the most powerful coping strategy I've begun learning. I may never be quite as humble as I want or need to be, but I can honestly say that my humility is growing. And as my humility grows, so also grows my ability to calmly deal with situations that, a few years ago, would have filled me with either fear or indignant rage.

I am sure age, an array of experiences, an increased sense of the importance of humility and bio feedback have all played a part in my increased ability to handle new and stressful circumstances, but I think the most critical piece of the puzzle is a stronger awareness of my relationship with the God of my understanding. This relationship played a major role in my having peace during my Cancer experience.

For nearly a decade, I haven't had to turn to drugs or drink to deal with negative defeated thoughts. Remembering the troubles the divine presence has already brought me through, and the peace and stability I'm connected with reminds me that all things work together for good to those who trust that the God or higher power of their understanding is watching over them.

A popular greeting card attributes this quote to Henry David Thoreau: "Happiness is like a butterfly: the more you chase it, the more it will elude you, but if you turn your attention to other things, it will come and sit softly on your shoulder."

With all due respect to Thoreau, that isn't the way I see it. According to a growing number of psychologists, you can *choose* to be happy. You can chase down that elusive butterfly and get it to sit on your shoulder. How? -- In part, by simply making the effort to monitor the workings of your mind.

Some people worry that wanting to be happier is a selfish goal, but research shows that happier people are more sociable, likable, healthy, and productive—and they're more inclined to help other people. By working to boost your own happiness, you're making other people happier, too.

There is no better time than now for you to allow yourself to be happy. It is time to embrace yourself and all that you have to offer. Be alone; give yourself the chance to learn about yourself, expand your soul and allow yourself to grow. Enable each chapter of your life to help you become a better you. Press forward, putting one foot in front of the other, until you are finally so overwhelmingly confident that you can look back, and see that you have climbed mountains.

CHAPTER 27

Kicking Worry to the Curb

Sorrow looks back, Worry looks around and Faith looks up.
— Ralph Waldo Emerson

*I am an old man and have known a great many troubles,
but most of them have never happened.*
— Mark Twain

DO YOU FIND YOURSELF CONSTANTLY WORRYING about something, anything and EVERYTHING? Has anyone ever told you, *"I don't have to worry; you do enough of it for both of us!"* Have you been identified as a worry wart or a nervous Nellie? If this sounds like you, then you may be worrying your life away. This excessive worry doesn't just affect our mental health; it also can wreak havoc on our physical well-being.

And all of us worry about the same things, everything from work and school to health and relationships. What separates us as a worrier from someone who is calm isn't the content of our thoughts it's the connotation of our thinking.

How we feel is often affected by the company we keep, whether we're aware of it or not. Studies show that emotions are contagious. We can quickly "catch" moods from other people—even from strangers who never speak a word (e.g. the terrified woman sitting by you on the plane; the fuming man in the checkout line). The people we spend a lot of time with have an even greater impact on our mental state.

Worry saps our energy and leaves us feeling tense. It interferes with our lives: we have to plan for it, we give in to it, we accommodate it and it pushes us to avoid situations where we know it will get worse. Often we are so used to carrying the burden of worry that we forget how much it is impacting on our lives - it has become so habitual that we no longer even notice.

Worry is often described as a chain of negative thoughts, images and doubts about things that might happen in the future. In essence, worriers tend to be concerned about what's 'around the corner' rather than what's here right now. So, for the most part, worry is not about things where the outcome is *certain*, it's about things where the outcome is *uncertain*.

Worrying doesn't always deserve such a bad rap. Sometimes worry is a good thing. If there is an actual threat then there is something to worry about. If you run into a bear in the woods, you have something to worry about, even if you have someone with you who runs slower than you. In these cases not worrying may be more of a problem than worrying.

So how much worry is too much worry? It depends on the degree to which that disproportionate worry affects you and how much you are suffering and how much it limits you. If it's posing interference in your life or is enough of a problem or nuisance that you are distressed, the good news is that there is help.

Short-term anxiety can be useful. Feeling nervous before I make a speech in front of a large audience can make me feel more alert, and enhance my performance. However, if the feelings of anxiety are overwhelming, my ability to concentrate and do well, may suffer.

Ultimately, worrying is simply negative thinking. The crazy part is that your brain doesn't know the difference between a positive and a negative thought, which means you can take control of those worrisome thoughts that possess our mind!

The 'fight or flight' reflex: Anxiety and fear can protect us from danger. When we feel under threat, anxiety and fear trigger the release of hormones, such as adrenalin. Adrenalin causes our heart to beat faster to carry blood where it's most needed. We breathe faster to provide the extra oxygen required for energy. We sweat to prevent overheating. Our mouth may feel dry as our digestive system slows down to allow more blood to be sent to our muscles. Our senses become heightened and your brain becomes more alert.

These changes make our bodies able to take action and protect us in a dangerous situation either by running away or fighting. It is known as the 'fight or flight' reflex. Once the danger has passed, other hormones are released, which may cause you to shake as your muscles start to relax.

We're not powerless over our worry and anxiety. We can move forward by limiting our negative thinking. Below is a list of things that add to our anxiety, worry and stress.

NEGATIVE THINKING

All-or-nothing thinking - Looking at things in black-or-white categories, with no middle ground. "If I fall short of perfection, I'm a total failure."

Overgeneralization - Generalizing from a single negative experience, expecting it to hold true forever. "I didn't get hired for the job. I'll never get any job."

The mental filter - Focusing on the negatives while filtering out all the positives. Noticing the one thing that went wrong, rather than all the things that went right.

NEGATIVE THINKING
Diminishing the positive - Coming up with reasons why positive events don't count. "I did well on the presentation, but that was just dumb luck."
Jumping to conclusions - Making negative interpretations without actual evidence. You act like a mind reader, "I can tell she secretly hates me." Or a fortune teller, "I just *know* something terrible is going to happen."
Catastrophizing - Expecting the worst-case scenario to happen. "The pilot said we're in for some turbulence. The plane's going to crash!"
Emotional reasoning - Believing that the way you feel reflects reality. "I feel frightened right now. That must mean I'm in real physical danger."
'Should's' and 'should-nots' - Holding yourself to a strict list of what you should and shouldn't do and beating yourself up if you break any of the rules
Labeling – Labeling yourself based on mistakes and perceived shortcomings. "I'm a failure; an idiot; a loser."
Personalization - Assuming responsibility for things that are outside your control. "It's my fault my son got in an accident. I should have warned him to drive carefully in the rain."

Healthy worry helps us survive by either avoiding danger or by preparing for it. But unnecessary worry can also give us ulcers and make us unproductive time wasters, especially if we worry about things that cannot be changed.

Worrying is seen as a way to predict what the future has in store—a way to prevent unpleasant surprises and control the outcome. The only problem is, it doesn't work.

Thinking about all the things that could go wrong doesn't make life any more predictable. You may feel safer when you're worrying, but it's just an illusion. Focusing on worst-case scenarios won't keep bad things from happening. It will only keep you from enjoying the good things you have in the present. So if you want to stop worrying, start by tackling your need for certainty and immediate answers.

What is worry? Worry is the act of becoming immobilized in the present as a result of things that are going, or are not going to happen in the future. Worry is like being in a rocking chair. It will give you something to do, but it won't get you anywhere.

Worry becomes a major problem because of our ability to imagine different scenarios about what just might happen. These different scenarios can be especially worrisome because of our tendency to focus on negative possibilities.

Imagination sets people apart from animals by helping us invent everything from rockets, to HD televisions, to subprime mortgages. Imagination can also create problems for us when we worry about things that may never happen and that we have no control of anyway.

Unskilled Worry: Unskilled worry is why the worry Attitude has such a bad reputation. Producers of anti-depressants, anti-anxiety and anti-psychotic medications, as well as cigarettes and alcohol, owe a large part of their profits to our human tendency to be unskilled worriers. An unskilled worrier is someone whose imagination has run amok.

Not everyone turns to unhealthy vices to deal with stress. Some deal with stress by exercising their religious faith. Praying to a higher power can be like a port in the storm of life. But while a person's idea of God may be a viable alternative to addictions, a person's relationship with the God of their understanding can also be a Band-Aid they use instead of learning to properly use their imaginations and "worry muscles."

To me, learning how to properly use our imaginations and worry muscles is a far healthier option than covering our concern with medication, with self-serving relationships with other worriers or even with another person's idea of the divine. Until I developed my own idea of the divine and my own relationship with the divine, the amount of strength and peace I could get from the divine was affected by whatever potential problems my imagination conjured up for me to worry about.

Skillful Imagining: A person whose imagination has run amok is like a kayaker who focuses on the rocks speeding by or an extreme skier who focuses on the trees instead of the spaces between the trees.

Focusing on the rocks and trees or other life problems is playing with the awesome power of suggestion and is misusing our incredibly creative imaginations. If we give in to our natural tendency to focus on problems, we'll have plenty to focus on. If we choose to focus on possibilities and opportunities, we'll have even more to focus on. Choosing what you'll focus on is called Living On Purpose.

For me, it was impossible to quit focusing on what could go wrong until I learned steps that put the worry habit to rest. So many people are unhealthy worriers that the subject has been studied and written about at great length.

The following four keys to eliminating worry are a combination of tools I have found useful and things written by Wayne Dyer and revered spiritual teacher Deepak Chopra.

1. **Begin to view the present moment as a time to live,** rather than to obsess about the future. When you catch yourself worrying, ask, "What am I avoiding now by using up this moment with worry?" Then begin to take action on what you are avoiding.

2. **Recognize the preposterousness of worry.** Ask yourself over and over, "Is there anything that will change as a result of my worrying about it?" For example: Will my worrying affect the stock market or the weather? Will my worrying affect whether or not my child has an accident?

3. **Give yourself shorter and shorter periods of "worry time."** Designate 10 minutes in the morning to worry—and when that time has elapsed, refuse to worry until your afternoon worry segment.

4. **Make a worry list of everything you worried about** yesterday or last year, and then see if your worry did anything to affect the outcome.

It makes no sense to worry about the things you have no control over, since you have no control over them, anyway. And also, it makes no sense to worry about the things you do have control over, because you have control over them. And there goes everything that it is possible to worry about. Either you have control or you don't, and worry is just a waste of your precious present.

Worry is a negative thought. We need a positive thought to replace it with. If you can't think of a positive thought, find someone to do something for and watch their reaction.

Worry thoughts can dampen the joy in our days. They can amplify our anxiety and spike our stress. Fortunately, we have many tools to help us step off the hamster wheel of swirling worries, and solve our problems, relax and enjoy life.

The more positive thoughts and memories we store up from inspirational biographies, personal experiences, songs or friends, the easier it will be to let go of the negative and welcome the positive. And when we celebrate our abilities, we'll look for the possibilities in situations where we used to find limitations.

Remember, there are *NO LIMITS*, except those we believe in.

CHAPTER 28

Living with Purpose

Challenging the meaning of life is the truest expression
of the state of being human.
—Vicktor E. Frankl

WHY ARE WE HERE ON THIS EARTH? What is our true purpose in life? These questions have plagued philosophers and ordinary folks for centuries.

Viktor Frankl's central theme was the necessity of finding purpose in life. As he tells the powerful story in *Man's Search for Meaning,* he learned having a purpose was the only way to survive the tortures of a Nazi concentration camp.

He identified three ways of finding meaning in one's life. They are work, love and the one he believed was most important, the ability to rise above oneself.

When faced with tragedy and situations that were unalterable, he believed that a person could escape the feeling of being a helpless victim. The key was to find meaning in the suffering itself and to define a guiding purpose that could change the direction of one's life.

Thrown into the midst of the worst torture and suffering imaginable, subject to arbitrary "selection" for death, living through the grueling work details and lack of food only by mastery of the small tricks of survival, he learned the lesson that would shape his later life and career.

Without a sense of purpose, no one could live for long in those camps. He saw the truth that starkly. Those who could believe in a positive future, or even a single event like liberation from the camp, and who could sustain the will to achieve it, lived. Those who lacked that inner sense of purpose and meaning died. Those who held such an idea in mind could live as long as it lasted. Once it was lost or given up, they died. Learning the art of survival was not enough; there had to be a vision of what came next that transcended all the suffering.

Frankl developed the basis of his psychiatric practice from such extreme experience. He believed – and I share that belief – that all of us need a sense of meaning and purpose not just for bare survival but for fulfillment as human beings. Since I have survived after my motorcycle crash and 34 years of living with a disability that sense of meaning and the hope it engenders must have been much stronger than I imagined.

Getting beyond survival, beyond the goal of recovery – that's where I am now, shaping a new future while trying to make the most of the life that fills and surrounds me. What sense do you have of the role of will and purpose in getting past depression?

Finding purpose in life that goes beyond our personal needs is often mentioned as a major step in overcoming depression. That's a hard thing to imagine, though, when we're in the middle of a severe relapse, and survival is the only goal in sight.

Yet, one of the hallmarks of depression is loss of motivation to do anything because we may feel that our life is meaningless. *We* are meaningless, empty, worthless, bad, nothing but a burden. There's no sense of future, no purpose to give us hope and help pull us back to an active life.

A sense of purpose goes along with building hope for the future, hope for recovering from depression and getting your life back. Even though we can't focus on it when we're struggling, hope and purpose are basic for regaining a sense of who we are.

Victor Frankl said that the fundamental drive in human existence is the need to find meaning in life in general, not just in your life. He calls this *transcendent or divine* meaning, one that includes us in a greater whole.

Many find this greater meaning and purpose in God and spirituality or service to country or activism for social good. Frankl believes that having a sense of purpose and self-fulfillment are the by-products of attempting to fulfill a larger meaning. Putting yourself into an activity that goes beyond you can make the difference between just getting by and feeling fully alive again.

With that being said, also remember that our worth is not proportional to what we achieve in life. Part of depressive thinking and our inner critical voice keeps telling us that it is and that we always fall short. This is a classic example of *all or nothing thinking*, and it's an ever-present danger for the battered self-esteem.

How do we find this larger purpose if we feel we don't have one? Starting at any level is important, and support groups build on our own need for help. We may look at them only as a means to feel better ourselves, but what we're doing is helping ourselves by helping others.

What drew me into it was the concerned and non-judgmental response I got the first time I spoke up about my problems. As the group continued to meet over time, we would share the good feeling when one of us made progress and empathize with anyone having a tough time. We had all had similar experiences, and that helped us talk freely.

This may not sound like finding a meaning in life. That phrase suggests a great epiphany, a call from on high to some noble duty. But the reality is down to earth. You start at a level that feels good and supportive and see where you go from there.

Alcoholics Anonymous has always understood the power of one addict helping another. Both are supported and both are doing something that goes beyond their immediate personal need. That's why service became one of the three pillars of recovery from AA's earliest days.

I doubt you can live without a belief that there is some purpose to your life. It's so common to hear people say that they want to make a difference. They want recognition, but they also want a sense that they're doing something that will help others as well.

This may be the farthest thing from your mind when you're absorbed in a depression nightmare. But I feel it's one of those anchor points I need so that I can look ahead with hope.

Does this idea make sense in your work to get rid of depression? Have you been able to find a meaning and purpose that helps you keep your bearings during the worst moments?

Why does it matter whether or not your life actually has a purpose? Let's take a few steps back and creep up on this question....

If you complete a task, and there's no overall important context for that task, then the task doesn't really matter. So you watch a TV show. It doesn't make a difference — there's no larger context for it. But if you complete a task that's part of a larger project, now it suddenly matters, at least within the context of the project. If you create a web page, and it's a part of a new web site you're building, that task matters. It takes you closer to the realization of the completed project.

Now when does a project matter? Projects matter only within the context of a larger goal. If your goal is to increase your income, and you complete a project that is likely to facilitate it, the project matters. It brings you a step closer to the realization of your goal. But if you complete a project like digging a trench through your backyard, and there's no real goal you're trying to accomplish, then the project is pointless. There's no meaning behind it.

For me, simple projects put together, made a big difference for my goal to become more independent. One sunny spring day, long after discovering the adaptive strength of accepting myself and my disability, I gripped my walking stick, hobbling and limping through a beautifully wooded section of a national park. Feeling somewhat philosophical, I wondered about the well-known story of the purpose of an oak tree.

The Oak's Purpose is to Grow: Let's take a look at the life of an oak tree. It starts as an acorn. It is warmed by the spring sun, the falling rains, and dark nights. Deep inside it starts growing. Finally, the stress of being pent up in a little shell is greater than its fear of what's outside. Tentatively, at first, it starts to grow. As the seasons pass, it gets bigger and stronger.

The oak is battered by the typical storms of life. One storm is so severe the tree is disabled, a huge limb torn away by lightning. What does it do then? Does it curl up and refuse to grow, or will it adapt? Without a thought, it absolutely adapts.

It continues to live, to grow, putting more and more energy into the limbs that remain. In time, it produces acorns that will produce more oak trees. So what is the oak tree's purpose? It seems that the oak's purpose is to be the best, biggest, greenest, healthiest oak that it can be in the situation in which it finds itself. In this state, it is best suited to provide food and shelter to forest denizens.

It's About Growing Toward Our Purpose: Holding my cane squarely in front of me, I lean forward on it and look down a large hill, over miles of lush green trees and bushes. A charred, partially rotted stump injects the reality of death. Tiny new plants growing in the rich nutrients of the decaying stump testify that its existence has always been about growth, first its own. The bigger it got the more food and shelter it provided. In death, its existence is still about growth, the growth of others.

One definition of life is growth. When we stop growing, we start decaying. But, through our legacies and through books, films, memoirs and journals we can still pass on wisdom to grow by, to live on, to generations that come behind us.

When I apply this meaning of life to things I come across, it makes sense. Our purposes in life do not change because we become rich or poor, disabled or athletic, Christian or Atheist, fat or thin or any other thing. Our purpose is to nourish the lives around us—whether our own offspring or others. The lesson of the oak tree shows that growing and evolving and helping others do the same is what life has always been about.

Consider a grove of ancient oak trees. To a member of the British or Irish priestly class, the Druids, oaks could represent a sacred place of worship. To a craftsman, they may represent a table or a chair; to a logger, they may mean a day's work. In short, life has the meaning you or I give it.

Disabilities Change Nothing: Disabilities or any other challenges we face, regardless of their significance, have little to do with whether or not we recognize and fulfill our purpose. As I grow old enough to consider past choices, I'm realizing that we're held accountable by ourselves, if no one else, for the ways we spend our time. Since I've recognized and begun pursuing my purpose like it's a responsibility instead of something silly or vague, life seems so much richer.

How will your eulogy read?

I imagine I'm at a funeral. It doesn't matter if it's in a church, chapel or crematorium. I wander in a bit late. The place is fairly full. I sit on the side and look around and recognize a sea of familiar faces. The service starts. Suddenly it strikes me—this is my funeral! My best friend stands to give the eulogy.

My interest is captured. I pay strict attention to what she might say. Will she say what I hope she says? Will she say that I lived as though growing and contributing to the growth of others were sacred responsibilities? Will she say I cared about others?

I'm not a know-it-all expert; far from it, I'm brain damaged. I procrastinate, I can't help it. I get distracted by many unimportant projects, and shiny objects. I'm not as disciplined as I'd like to be.

But because I'm a relentless observer of what makes for a remarkable life, I have discovered what it takes to lead a life that counts. Judging from some of the people I've met who live with a sense of regret and hopelessness, it's obvious that we often make mistakes in the pursuit of a meaningful life. But it doesn't have to be that way.

My defined purpose is to *live consciously and courageously, to resonate with love and compassion, to awaken the great spirits within others, and to leave this world in peace.* To clarify what this means to me, I arranged it in the following chart. Sharing my physical and emotional experience, strength and hope all over the US and Canada is one project that fulfills my purpose in life.

Live consciously	Be aware of how my words and actions affect myself and others.
...and courageously.	Be humble enough to make amends when I say or do something that hurts someone.
Resonate with love.	Loving others is the best way to receive love.
Have compassion.	Have concern for others that is based on their comfort and not my expectations.
Awaken the possibilities within others.	Remember that a true winner treats others like they're winners, too.
Live in peace by learning from the oak.	The oak's purpose is to grow strong and to contribute to the growth of others.

In a nutshell, my purpose is to:

Knowing and accepting my purpose makes life a lot more meaningful. Regardless of the fortunate or the unfortunate things that have happened to me, I have a purpose. There's a reason to get up and do my best each day. My purpose is bigger than me. It's to contribute to the growth of everyone in my life.

We'll always have pressing concerns to address if we want to survive in this world, because life is tough.

Life will continually tell you that you can't do it. That it's too tough or even impossible. But if you're purposely living with a purpose, step back and listen carefully. You'll hear HOPE whispering: "Keep trying. You can do it. Remember: ***Winners Don't Quit!***"

CHAPTER 29

Following Mentors and Role Models

We're here for a reason. I believe a bit of the reason
is to throw little torches out to lead people through the dark.
—Whoopi Goldberg

BY NOW I HAVE STARTED TO UNDERSTAND the incredible gift of mentors and role models. Learning from someone who is older and or wiser and who really cares about teaching me how to succeed as a speaker, author and person is one of the greatest gifts I've ever been given.

In the beginning, I did a lot more receiving than I did giving, but as time has gone on and as I've begun making money and acquiring additional teachers, I've begun paying my teachers and mentors. My highest hope, a hope that I anticipate realizing one day, is that I will be able to pass this gift on to others. I have not yet reached the stage where I feel comfortable enough with my own knowledge to think that I would make a valuable mentor in any but the simplest matters, but there are two things I've learned that you may find useful:

Find and attach yourself to someone you can learn from and who can help you grow toward being the type of person you admire.

Whether they realize it or not, everyone has an inner spiritual yearning. On the outside, they may claim to be Buddhist, Muslim, Christian, Hindu or they may claim something else. The most important thing to realize is that nobody can prove that they are right and somebody else is wrong, so I won't tell you what to believe. I appreciate the same consideration.

For years, I have intentionally sought out mentoring and role-model relationships—someone to whom I could attach myself, someone that could help me both see and realize my potential. Not every relationship worked. Some did. Some did not. As in any healthy relationship, there must be mutual fulfillment. It is this mutual fulfillment that defines a good mentoring relationship. A good mentoring relationship is honest about motivations.

What do mentors look for in a person in whom they will invest themselves? Seven characteristics suggest themselves to me:

1. Unrealized potential, undeveloped possibilities
2. Curiosity and a hunger to learn
3. Strength of character
4. Shared values in life
5. Reflective thinking and self-assessment
6. Willingness to accept responsibility for one's growth
7. Energy, purpose and hope

There are also seven characteristics I always seek in a prospective mentor:

1. Wisdom
2. Strength of character
3. Shared values
4. Accumulated experiences
5. Continued learning
6. Reflective articulation on life
7. Accessibility

It is the character of the person that draws us to mentors. Mentors have character—they are characters —they live out the commitments of their character.

The following is a list of people I have learned from. Many of them are family or friends, but some of them are people I have never met.

> ### *Grandma Moses: Late Bloomer*
> *Life is what you make it. Always has been, always will be.*

The world renowned American Folk artist Grandma Moses is often cited as an example of an individual successfully beginning an art career late in life. Grandma Moses has snapped me out of more than one state of lethargy. By seeing the career she built in her 70s, I realize the sky's the limit.

When you have a disability like I have, you feel like you're always behind where you wish to be. Realizing that Grandma Moses didn't achieve all that she was capable of until her 70s puts her in my "A" list of role-model favorites. During the 1950s, her exhibitions were so popular that they broke attendance records all over the world. At age 88, *Mademoiselle* Magazine named Grandma Moses as the "Young Woman of the Year."

> ### *Neil Young: Determination and Humanitarian*
> *Once you've been to hell and back,*
> *the things the rest of us find anxiety-inducing*
> *—the scary odds against making it as an artist,*
> *for example—aren't all that scary.*

One man I admire for not letting his own condition stand in the way of his success—and for his obvious dedication to people with disabilities—is the Canadian-born singer song writer widely regarded as one of the most influential musicians of his generation. Of course I'm talking about Neil Young.

The casual listener and fan may not be aware that Neil Young is yet another famous musician who has disabilities. In 1951 at the age of six, Young contracted polio. Since childhood he's reportedly had diabetes and epilepsy. In 2005 he had successful surgery for a brain aneurysm. He also has two sons with cerebral palsy. Like Young himself, his daughter Amber suffers from epilepsy.

In 1986 he and his wife started the Bridge School in San Francisco, a learning center for children with disabilities. A 1989 alternative rock compilation album raised money for the school. So, those are Young's numerous "credentials." His song, *"Helpless"* is about his experience with childhood polio.

I don't know every detail of Neil Young's life. I don't need to in order to be inspired in specific areas of my life. I'm inspired most of all by two of Neil Young's qualities or accomplishments.

- ☐ His ability to overcome his disabilities and become a rock and roll hall of fame legend.

- ☐ His work for people with disabilities makes him one of my personal heroes.

Mickey Mantle: Perseverance
If I knew I was going to live this long, I'd have taken better care of myself.

During practice for a high school football game, Mantle was accidentally kicked on the left shin. The wound developed into the bone disease *osteomyelitis*.

It became so serious doctors wanted to amputate Mickey's leg. His mother wouldn't hear of it and his dad Mutt drove Mickey 175 miles to the *Crippled Children's Hospital* in Oklahoma City. They saved the leg but his legs were in such bad shape, the army wouldn't take him. His legs kept him in constant pain. He had to wrap them in bandages before every ball game.

Knowing the high price Mantle paid to be one of the baseball's all-time greatest players, gives me the drive and the tolerance to be my best even when it would be easier to quit.

Jack Dempsey: Brave and Courageous
A Champion is someone who gets up when he can't.

Jack Dempsey held the boxing World Heavyweight Championship from 1919 to 1926. His fights set financial and attendance records, including the first million dollar gate, but that didn't impress me much. What I couldn't forget is what he said: "A Champion is someone who gets up when he can't."

As I used to hobble around the block, falling every once in a while, I kept thinking to myself: *"A champion, a survivor, is someone who gets up when he can't."*

Stephen Hawking: Genius with a Disability
If you are disabled, it is probably not your fault, but it is no good blaming the world or expecting it to take pity on you. One has to have a positive attitude and must make the best of the situation that one finds oneself in; if one is physically disabled, one cannot afford to be psychologically disabled as well. I find that people in general are very ready to help, but you should encourage them to feel that their efforts to aid you are worthwhile by doing as well as you possibly can.

As of 2012, Hawking is almost completely paralyzed and communicates through a speech-generating device. I love Hawking's attitude as he describes himself as lucky, despite his disease. He says he has not been hindered from having, in his own words, "a very attractive family."

Hawking himself proves that: Attitude is everything. And that, my friend, is what it's been all about. When I see someone like Steve Hawking pushing through his disability boundaries, I know I can, too.

Katherine Peil: Soul Sister

I'm a well-kept secret I hope to share. What Katherine is REALLY doing at any given moment: Trying to build a language to express simple yet ineffably abstract naturalistic realities, ideas that remain obscured within pretentious linguistic traditions, misguided cultural assumptions, overly analytical and unruly synthetic academic standards, and limited scientific models. Just shoot me now.

—Katherine Peil

Katherine graduated from Harvard University in 2009 in Science and Religion, an expert in the role of emotion in "naturalistic spirituality" in Cambridge, Massachusetts. Wow, what an intellectual powerhouse she is, but more importantly, she is spiritually mature and kind, and always has been.

The first time I met Katherine was on the bus. Our memories differ significantly before reuniting, so I will let her tell it from here. (Apparently, a Harvard degree gives more credibility than considerably noticeable brain damage.)

"Spirituality, to me, is about the serendipitous creativity of the universe and our rich experience as conscious, connected, co-creators. A deep truth for me is that when the universe delivers a painful challenge, it also embodies a potential spiritual gift – the worse the challenge, the more profound the gift. Indeed, I have always has a particular respect for those who have faced the most difficult

challenges, and have not only survived, but have transcended them with their integrity intact.

Likewise, I have always been drawn to the creatively eccentric, and those on outskirts of human normalcy—those with genetic anomalies, mystical sensitivities or boundary defying sojourns of consciousness, or with obvious behavioral aberrations. The outliers on the Bell Curve, those who are all-too-easy to ignore as different, those who it is often considered impolite to even look at. But my work suggests that such polity is actually little more than a self-serving excuse to hide from our own fears, to resist the empathic truth that what has happened to them could happen to us. So such heroic folks deserve and claim a special place in my heart.

I met such a person back in the early 90's, while commuting on the Metro bus across the lake to the University of Washington. He was a young man (perhaps in his mid-to-late twenties), sitting alone yet engaged in a highly animated discussion with himself. Although the bus was crowded there were many conspicuously empty seats surrounding him, perhaps because such folks oftentimes take offense when a stranger interrupts the in-depth conversation, under the mistaken assumption that the verbal flow is intended to solicit social jibber-jabber. Indeed, this particular young man was largely unintelligible, with both his movements and speech suggesting he'd had far too much to drink. Still, something about him haunted me into his sphere to say hello.

He responded immediately, seemingly starved for human contact, and with tremendous enthusiasm (yet truly terrible elocution) regaled me for nearly two hours with details of a book he was writing – a novel for teens, with an intricately detailed plot and a distinctively named protagonist. What I found particularly charming was his humble apology for his labored speech.

As if it were an aside, he explained that he was just returning from a physical therapy session – one of an endless series that had followed a horrific motor cycle accident he had had endured more than a decade earlier, at the tender age of 19. That's the real story here, I recall thinking. No Kidding. For as I would later discover, he had suffered severe brain damage, was partially paralyzed, including his larynx, and that he had been told he would never walk or talk again.

Yet here he was, years later, riding alone on the bus, writing a book and brimming with hope and enthusiasm. I told him I found his ambition most inspiring, after witnessing others who - under far more fortunate circumstances - talked endlessly about writing, but never really produced. He responded with surprise, asking something like: "What else would I be doing", having a paid off condo and with all this free time?"... as if grateful for his accident.

At that moment, it was clear to me that here before me, shining forth from a broken, twisted, lump of physical flesh, sat the most indomitable spirit I had perhaps ever experienced.

Our chance meeting had occurred at high point in my own life, while sailing along a promising educational track toward a PhD in Psychology. But it was a path that would be diverted shortly thereafter due to a rather dreadful series of my own challenges, those that would land me several years later in a stop-gap food-on-my-children's-table job cutting hair in a cut-rate little chop-shop. One morning, out of the blue, in the door stumbles an odd young man, walking with a pronounced lurch, and shouting in slurred speech at the startled receptionist:

"I WANT KATHERINE!" (Something I was rather alarmed to hear from across the crowded, now curious, room.) I excused myself from my client and intercepted him as he headed my way; already declaring (quite boisterously) that his mother had recommended me as a high quality but "cheap deal."

I shook my finger at him, smiled cautiously and said: "I know you. We met on the bus a few years ago, and you were writing a book, a novel about a young fellow named Tigue." A wave of dawning recognition began to cross his face along with the most amazing and surely heartfelt smile. And at that moment he imprinted upon me like a young duckling; shamelessly stalking me for free haircuts and sisterly favors – such as darning his socks, guiding and editing his writing, and commandeering my free time for general emotional support.

But he was clearly a soul brother, hand delivered – twice – by the universe to my door, and he responded zealously to my vision of him; flowering as if even my frenzied annoyance and brutal kindred honesty were spiritual nourishment. And perhaps they were. For our chance meeting had occurred at a turning point in his life, and our spiritual synergy happened to tip things in a certain direction. Indeed, I recall lamenting early on (during perhaps the first free haircut, with Al swathed in a cutting gown out on my deck).

"You know Al, you are a very high-maintenance friend." To which he responded—without missing a beat: "Well when you own a Mercedes, you have to wash it every day!" He said it with such soulful self-assurance as to strike at the very core of humility itself. So upon recovering from the first of many belly laughs to come, I told him he was very funny, and that he should use his humor in order to help share his personal story.

And, as they say, the rest is history!

Al Foxx is indeed a very special soul; the very embodiment of the spiritually divine creative spark, and a beacon to help it kindle and shine forth from within his fellow humans. And it has been a tremendous honor and pleasure to answer my call as his soul sister.

With love, Katherine Peil, 9-24-2012"

That's her version, and as I said, her credibility platform outranks my own, so we'll go with it. Katherine gave me confidence by being interested enough in me and my budding comedy career to come to some of my shows.

Realizing I needed a little polishing, she bought me a blazer to wear on stage and made me feel appreciated by being interested in me and my progress. Katherine and I share a commonality of purpose adding something special for each other in this world.

I heard someone say, "Some friends are for a reason and some are for a season." I found that not to be at all true of a real friend like Katherine.

Mark Robertson: Friend like a Brother
It takes some children years to realize they're orphans and then years to decide to be adopted.

Whether you go to a mosque, a synagogue, a church or a shrine, I hope it gives you what you feel like you need. Since 1999, Northshore Baptist Church has been my source of peace and many positive relationships. One of the first people I got to know at Northshore Baptist Church was Mark Robertson. He's a teacher at a public high school where I have been blessed to share my strategy for overcoming challenges and living a happy and useful life.

One of the things that attracted me to Mark is his sometimes zany sense of humor. Another of his gifts that I enjoy is his musical ability.

Something he and our very good friend Roger enjoy getting together and playing their guitars and banjos. The timing hasn't yet been right for me, but I'm looking forward to accepting Mark's invitation to bring my harmonica over and join their musical extravaganza. I am happy to have a good friend like Mark who is genuinely a good person.

> **Jan Hettinga: Spiritual Advisor**
> *Struggling to change outward habits without changing the heart*
> *is a formula for frustration.*

There are so many different beliefs, none of which can be proven to someone who believes something else that I want it clearly understood that I am not inviting you to believe any certain way. I found something that works for me, and I hope what you have works for you.

Jan Hettinga is the founder and was the senior pastor of the Northshore Baptist Church for over two decades. He was my pastor for a decade. Pastor Hettinga mentored me with his encouragement in my spiritual life as well as my speaking career. I had regular weekly meetings with him for many months, while he assisted me in developing my *"Sing Anyway"* presentation, a message I have shared with many churches.

Pastor Jan blessed me with his incredible wisdom and valuable time, by improving my leadership, organizational and communication skills of which I feel truly appreciative. His support and confidence in me made a big difference in my life for which I am grateful.

> **Steve Michiels: Spiritual Advisor**
> *Giving a message is more than just having a message.*
> *Giving a message includes being the message.*

The associate pastor at Northshore Baptist, Steve Michiels, was also a very valuable mentor who taught me that giving a message is more than just having a message. Giving a message includes acting in such a way that you are the message.

His many hours of guidance through some of my personal relationships, improved my awareness of my own learning gaps. Pastor Steve provided the support and counsel I needed and that made a big difference in my life, for which I am grateful.

> **Bob Rorabaugh: Spiritual Advisor**
> *I really appreciate that Al's a brother in Christ who keeps us laughing.*

Another mentor and pastor from Northshore Baptist, Bob Rorabaugh, is the planner of our annual Whacky Wheelays event. Bob has organized this event for many years for *people of all abilities. People bring all sorts of* wheeled contraptions. Everything from wheelchairs, wagons and bikes to pedal toys, trikes and scooters! The event is attended by local political leaders and fire departments and ends with an awards ceremony and a BBQ picnic and other festivities.

Bob, a good friend I spent a great deal of time walking with over the years. We've walked through most of the woods in area parks and greenbelts, talking about life and enjoying the fresh air. One of my fondest memories of Pastor Bob was when he surprised me, appearing out of nowhere to shake my hand after I won the 2,000 Laff-Off at Giggles Comedy Club in Seattle.

> **Rich Dover: How "Winners Don't Quit" Began**
> *Recovery is difficult. But it's absolutely possible,*
> *if Jesus is your higher power.*

Although I'm not pushing any particular spiritual belief, I'm not going to lie either. If a person with a particular belief helped in my rehab, or I see someone getting specific results through what they believe, I'll tell you like it was.

Rich is a Christian business man and web designer who built me my first website at a reduced cost. I had never heard of a website before meeting Rich. I was surprised and pleased with its power. Along with *countless* other activities, Rich worked as my agent for several years. He currently manages the recovery house: (www.fairhavenhouse.info). Rich made a big difference in my life and for that I am very grateful.

Thank you. Rich, for the incredible effort you put into my business and my life. Your business talent and leadership skill are beyond question.

Mike Rock: Dependable Strength
I'm batting a 1000. –**Mike Rock**
There is nothing on this earth more to be prized than true friendship.
—**Thomas Aquinas**

It pays to have a friend who's walked where you've walked and who has already gone through the spiritual and psychological changes you're going through. It pays because such a friend can strengthen your hope that there really is "light at the end of the tunnel." Mike is a friend who has been there and done that.

Being humble enough to learn from Mike's example over the past 7+ years, as he goes through good times and trials, has enriched and added much appreciated stability to my life. We have the kind of relationship that is mutually beneficial because of our open and honest conversations.

Mike has always allowed me to unburden my fears, listening and responding to me patiently and sympathetically. He's very knowledgeable about life, very much a common sense kind of man. I trust his good judgment on practical issues, even with my emotional feelings I may be struggling through. He consistently provides me positive ways to look at my challenges and makes them manageable.

Mike is a devout Catholic who loves and trusts the God of his understanding. Because of the principles that govern his life, Mike is as dependable as the day is long. Since I've been fortunate enough to have had some of his experiences as well as fortunate enough to not have had others, Mike offers me insights and wisdom I'm glad I don't have to live without.

Gus Henne: Owner **Forever Books Publishing**

To write what is worth publishing, to find honest people to publish it, and get sensible people to read it, are the three great difficulties
—Charles Caleb Colton

Forever Books is where I published my first, professionally edited, self-published book *No Limits.* Thanks to the guidance of owner Gus Henne, I discovered that writing a book makes you an expert. Another way to say that is: "A book is your key to the kingdom."

A good book is better than the best business card. My relationship with Gus was the first of its kind, for me. Through the internet, I'd get gigs all over the country. As part of the arrangement with the organization I was to speak for, I'd sell a number of my books. All I had to do was call up Gus and have the books shipped to wherever I planned to speak. The books would be waiting for me when I arrived.

I attended. I don't even remember where or exactly when it was. I regret to say that I'll never again hear Gus' calm and confident voice over the phone assuring me everything's taken care of. Gus was one of my friends cancer took.

Elaine Wright Colvin: Founder, Writers Info Network

There is nothing to writing.
All you do is sit down at a typewriter and bleed.
—Ernest Hemingway

As editor, writing instructor and publishing expert, Elaine played a big part in shaping and editing my first book, No Limits. When I found that other self-publishers were out of my budget, she introduced me to the owner of Forever Books Gus Henne who I just described.

Former student at Western Baptist Bible College, today a big part of Elaine's life is given to a missionary project called WIN India. I don't know many of the details, but I do know she and many of the others involved in this project spend much time bringing the hope of the Gospel and some of the essentials to living in this world to some of India's poorest inhabitants.

Thank you, Elaine. Your love of humanity and the generosity of your spirit was a blessing to me and is a blessing to many others.

Cheryl Peterson: Friend & WDQ Volunteer
If you think you can do a thing or think you can't do a thing, you're right.
—Henry Ford

Cheryl is amazing! Being the cost accountant for the Boeing store kept her busy, but not too busy to help me. To give you an idea how naturally gifted and intelligent she is just imagine experienced editors at a large writing conference finding it hard to believe she put together my one sheet with no prior writing experience.

Cheryl's remarkable insight and natural ability to figure things out and explain them made her a privilege to learn from. Our relationship went way beyond her helping me with writing projects and computer challenges. We did all kinds of things together.

"Good shot," I cheered as Cheryl's golf ball traveled over an intricate set of bumps and valleys before dropping in the hole.

"OK," she said. "That's two in a row. Let's get to the gym and home before Arianna gets there."

Eying Cheryl's profile on the way to 24 Hour Fitness, I breathe a prayer of thanksgiving. In many ways, she's more than a friend. She's a mentor and a role model.

Howard Howell: Social Media Expert
I have been blessed from the first day I met Al and became a recipient of his unique sense of humor and positive approach to life. I always enjoy our coaching sessions where Al inspires me more than I help him.
He helps me remain grounded in the appreciation
of the God given potential that we all have regardless
of our physical circumstances. Al is definitely a winner in my book.

Howard has been and is a very active national teacher who lives close enough to me for us to have in person consultations. He has helped me learn to navigate the social media world. Before learning the finer points of using my computer and the complex world of social media, I was like a baboon trying to understand the finer points of fly fishing.

Some teachers give us fish and some teach us how to fish. When someone is teaching you how to fish, hold on tight and learn all you can.

Patrick Snow: Author/Speaker & Coach
Only those who can see the invisible can achieve the impossible!

Writing and speaking requires having something to write and speak about, of course. But this is only the beginning. A piece of the puzzle that's just as important is having a method and a plan to tell folks you have something that will inform, entertain and or inspire them.

I've been to several of Patrick Snow's 3-day seminars. I soak up new information each time. It's not that the information is different each time; it's just that his seminars seem to me like I'm climbing a flight of stairs. I have to understand the first three stairs before I can take the next three. Another way to say it is that there's so much information that the more I hear, the more I add to what I've already learned.

Patrick is successful because he believes you only *get* out of life what you *give* to life. He has been generous and patient with me and I am grateful to have him on my team.

Wayne Jobskey: My Attitude Coach
Kindness is the language which the deaf can hear and the blind can see. —
—**Mark Twain**

When Wayne sees me, he smiles. He's my Attitude coach. Wayne is very limited in that he can only move his right hand and arm, though without much dexterity. He can't talk and he is unable to eat except by a tube to his stomach.

We play Blackjack. I deal him a card that he holds in his hand and then deal the other cards. I'm always talking when we're playing. Just stuff like "Look out Vegas, Wayne is back in town. Momma's getting a new pair of shoes tonight." I just keep it going and cheer Wayne on. Before I leave him each time, I tell him I love him and that he's helping a lot of people across the country because I talk about him as I travel to different states.

I also push Wayne's wheelchair around the square circular Life Care Center where he lives. I've been visiting him a couple years and everybody knows everybody. We stop in the physical therapy room and exercise the one arm he can move.

Today two friends from Toastmasters came with me to see Wayne. He loved the variety. When I visit Wayne, I tell him he's got a mission. I tell him that by keeping a strong Attitude and being my Attitude coach, he's helping more than just himself and me. He's helping thousands of folks he doesn't even know. Wayne smiles a lot. He's my Attitude coach.

Although I've known for most of my life that a person's Attitude is the key to either a happy or sad existence, clearly articulating that profound truth requires skills I had to learn.

My relationship with Wayne helps me keep the right Attitude. But I've also had to gain knowledge of how to shape and craft a talk that would share my experience and knowledge in an entertaining, informative and inspiring way.

> ### *Michael Buschmohle: International Trainer*
> *I've worked with Al Foxx for more than 10 years and he continues to amaze me. He has transformed his disabilities into an ability to reach into hearts, and with humor, to inspire everyone with his speaking and writing.*

President of Applause Associates and an international communications trainer, Michael has been mentoring me for well over 10 years, serving as a speech coach and editor of my presentations and books, as well as a graphic designer of some of my handouts and book covers. Michael is an author, editor, artist, speech writer, and media coach, college instructor in the U.S. and China, and trainer for Fortune 500 companies and government agencies.

He's a past hospital training director and a former Roman Catholic priest. Michael has helped brand me and shape my message.

Thank you for your help sir, Sir. I still have quite a ways to go before I'm what and where I want to be, but with the help of folks I'm blessed to be around reaching my goals is inevitable.

> ### *Bonnie Richter: Best Friend & Work Partner*
> *I respect Al because of his great attitude overcoming adversity.*
> *I enjoy Al because of his wonderful sense of humor.*
> *He is authentic and has an important message for all people.*

—**Bonnie Richter**

*A friend is someone who knows the song in your heart and can
sing it back to you when you have forgotten the words.*
—**Albert Camus**

Bonnie is my best friend and has had a significant and positive impact on the person I am becoming. She has become my "El Capitan." Having many years of experience as the Executive Director of a non-profit organization, she gives me very helpful advice in my business. She is my healthcare advocate and my social coach. Whenever I call her, I receive a friendly and kind voice that is ready to respond to any real needs. And when she calls me, I am there for her. She tells me I am her spiritual coach.

The relationship between Bonnie and I began when she happened to see me doing a New-Year's Eve comedy show in a casino. She contacted my agent and booked me to do some inspirational humor for the EMS organization where she served as executive director.

Luckily, the years between when I failed to lead in my relationship with Cheryl and now, that I have an opportunity to lead in my relationship with Bonnie, have seen much growth. I am not only mature enough to lead by principle rather than emotional or physical desire; I've also come to grips with the idea that it's not all about me.

Another fact in my favor is that Bonnie strongly believes in me and is committed to the mission of my non-profit organization Winners Don't Quit Association, which is inspiring people to believe in their own possibilities regardless of external circumstances and enabling people, with and without disabilities, to better understand each other.

Although I did my shows without using PowerPoint images, Bonnie suggested I try using PowerPoint for additional clarity and visual interest. Her idea to use illustrative images relevant to my current talk is proving to be a smashing success. Of course we do our best to use images that speak a thousand words without using a single word. People don't come to my talks so they can read; they come to hear me talk.

Bonnie also has a keen understanding of social protocol. When we go places together, I know my coach has my back, making sure I don't forget to thank someone and occasionally reigning in my rambunctious nature. She has been a blessing for me, polishing me with a more professional attitude and look. She gifted me with a very cool collection of hats that I'm continuously being complimented on. These Boston Travelers' Caps have become part of my trademark.

Bonnie was there for me from diagnosis through recovery of my cancer. She went to each doctor's appointment with me and asked all the important questions. She was tenacious, seeing that I got several opinions, before choosing the right doctor and treatment. She would read to me over the phone, chapter by chapter, making sure I understood the cancer and the many choices I needed to consider. She stayed in the hospital during my operation, getting update calls to her cell phone and sleeping on a cot they rolled in to my room.

Bonnie laughs at my jokes, even after hearing them countless times. When you think about the definition of friendship, I can't think of a better friendship than I've got with Bonnie. Even my parents have commented on the positive impact Bonnie has had on my work and my life. Bonnie is a gift that keeps on giving.

Fritz and Virginia Fuchs: My Parents

Making the decision to have a child is momentous. It is to decide forever to have your heart go walking around outside your body.
—Elizabeth Stone

> *We are proud of Al for what he has, through God's working in him, made of his life since his motorcycle accident. Instead of accepting that his paralysis and brain damage would keep him from doing much with his life, Al, by accepting his new life, discovered new and unexpected opportunities. He has worked untiringly to go from pointing out letters on an alphabet board to becoming an excellent public speaker helping others to overcome their own disabilities and crisis.*
> *Thank you, God, for your power to heal. We love you, Al.*
> **—Al's Mom and Dad, Fritz and Virginia Fuchs**
>
> *Give me the life of the boy whose mother is nurse, seamstress, washerwoman, cook, teacher, angel, and saint, all in one, and whose father is guide, exemplar, and friend. No servants to come between. These are the boys who are born to the best fortune.*
> **—Andrew Carnegie**

My amazing parents Fritz and Virginia have been and continue to be excellent role models. They've always provided me with a vision, a star to shoot for. They have always been there for me, consistently grounded and involved in my various chapters of life. My parents lean into each other and God for their strength, providing for me a template and a guiding light in my life's journey. How they have lived their life, writing happy endings, has provided me the compass I needed to write mine.

Words that say thank You Mom and Dad for all that you have done for me seem to fall far short of what I mean, but what else can you put in a book? Luckily we speak often enough for you to know what I really mean.

> ### *Harvey Fuchs: My Favorite Brother*
> *Growing up, Al and I were the definition of "sibling rivalry." He was the rebellious one everybody watched, while I got away with doing anything I wanted. Today, I admire Al. He doesn't quit when most people do, and he has the guts to share his costly wisdom.*
> **—Harvey Fuchs**

> *You can't have a better tomorrow if you are*
> *thinking about yesterday all the time.*
> **—Charles Kettering**

Harvey is my only sibling. Apparently, two boys were enough. During many of our years growing up, I was a nuisance to my younger brother. I have vivid recollections of times past. If I somehow got the chance to live my life over, in many ways, I would be more like my brother. He always had an interest in mechanical devices and little electric motors. With this interest and an aptitude in taking apart, and usually reassembling, a variety of mechanical objects, he went on to get a degree in industrial engineering and has worked at Boeing for 25 years and counting.

Our relationship traveled an evolutionary process through lessons-learned, strong parental leadership, and a shared family experience. Being more mature than I was in my younger years, I can admit that Harvey is a role model for me. By following at least most of the rules, he has accomplished a lot. He has worked in a variety of settings at Boeing for well over 20 years and has maintained a long and healthy marriage.

He has provided me with a wonderful sister-in-law who is a teacher and a niece that is a joy for anyone who knows her. He contributes greatly to his church and has always been there with a helping hand for my parents.

Thank you Harvey for all that you do for me and for Mom and Dad. I appreciate you. Watching your successes has given me the determination and the self- discipline to successfully own and operate my own speaking and writing business for 15 years.

There are a lot of things that happen that will drive us to lose our hope. Even when things seem hopeless, remember we have been given the greatest gift of all, the gift of life.

There are people who care and there are people who will help us. I encourage everyone to out there to find someone in your life that can mentor you and help you grow to be the best you can be.

Having a mentor can help us go through challenging life transitions. I have been very lucky to be around the right people for me to help make my dreams come true. Mentors already familiar with things I'm eager to learn have saved me massive amounts of time and give me a deeper understanding than I could ever get on my own.

And role models who exemplify behavior I admire and strive to emulate keep me focused on pursuing my goals. Because of the people I strive to be like, but mostly because of the people who instruct me in how to accomplish the practical things necessary to achieve my goals, I have a mission.

The most exciting part is that I am sometimes gradually and sometimes rapidly, but always, evolving into the type of person with a meaningful mission.

Achieving No Limits—Reach Goal after Goal: Reaching goals becomes habitual as you build up momentum. Especially if you're traveling the rehab road, I encourage you to set high goals and start planning how you're going to reach your next goal. It's never too early.

- ☐ What do you need to know and do to reach your next goal?
- ☐ Who or what can teach you what you need to know and do?
- ☐ What steps will prepare you to reach your goal?
- ☐ When are you going to start going for it?

Although mentors can fill any number of different roles, all mentors have the same goal in common: to help us to discover our strengths and to discover our potential.

Close, healthy, supportive relationships between mentors and mentees that last for a significant portion of time (i.e., more than one or two years) are central to success.

CHAPTER 30

Pushing Past Limitations

Do one thing every day that scares you.
— Eleanor Roosevelt

If you can't, you must. If you must, you can.
— Tony Robbins

MOST OF US DON'T KNOW OUR LIMITS, because we limit ourselves. We think we can't do something, even though deep down we really want to try. But then, we bring our limits into focus, or our limiting thoughts are just there, in the back of our minds, wearing us down.

Our friends and family sometimes contribute in bringing our doubts into focus, highlighting our inner doubts sometimes with faint praise, or platitudes, or even voicing our shortcomings directly. Our past behaviors limit us on what we want to do today, to become a better person. Sometimes the people closest to us doubt our possibilities, because of past negative conduct.

One of the best things about life is its consistency. As Grandma Moses said, "Life is what you make it. Always has been, always will be." So, I've had to push past my own voice of limitation, but also the doubting of my friends and family. Can I blame them? No, absolutely not! For quite a period of time in my life, one of my gifts was pushing the limits, but not in a positive way.

Self-control is an important skill for all *teenagers* to learn, and many adults as well. A person with self-control refers to having the power or control over one's own actions. At this point in my rehab, I was, in many ways, like a child who is still discovering the extent of his or her own power. Sometimes their power is misused, as was mine.

When we do certain things, we get certain results. When my self-esteem was at its lowest, I used the law of cause and effect, not purposely. In fact, I used it to my detriment. But, detriment or not, by using it, I proved that I still had some control over my situation. I would have been happier had I just trusted that the God of my understanding was going to work everything out.

But at the time, I couldn't just sit there. I had to control something, anything. Since my brain injury impacted everything, from my circumstances and emotions to my very body, the type of control I exerted was limited to trying to pull people into my life by being pleasant or pushing people out by being unpleasant.

Because being pleasant will pull people toward us only if they want to be pulled, pushing people away is much easier in terms of percentage of success. Without realizing it at the time, I was trying to restore a feeling of power over my limitations, so I did more pushing than pulling. I didn't understand this until a psychologist explained it to me. But even after hearing and understanding this explanation, I couldn't seem to stop pushing until I succeeded in pushing everybody, except my family, out of my life.

Combine my excessive drinking with a need for power and what you have is a candidate for Alcoholics Anonymous. The in-patient treatment center I mentioned earlier gave me certain tools and a basic understanding of why I drank. But as the years passed and I gradually began feeling better about my circumstances and myself, my need to drink changed.

Alcoholics Anonymous kept me clean and sober for four years. I continued going to AA when I returned to Walla Walla College, and as long as I did, that worked out fine. After being sober for a few years I decided to become a preacher and started going to Weimar College, a private seminary in California. Since spiritual people who were always talking about God surrounded me, I decided I didn't need to attend AA meetings anymore.

That mistake resulted in my giving in to the temptation to smoke a joint with a fellow pastoral ministry major who was evidentially fighting his own demons. Pot was my drug of choice, but once the door reopened, drinking and doing other things was a natural result. Deciding to be a pastor was an impulsive decision, which I didn't have the commitment to complete.

Instead, I returned to Seattle and made my second try at a four-year college. I've already mentioned how that went. One night at an open mic at a bar in south Seattle, I just happened to be the most experienced comic there, and the bartender said I was headlining and gave me an open bar tab. I got sloppy drunk, totally unprofessional. Promising myself to go slow and be careful, I decided to ignore the bartender's advice and drive home.

The bar was close to the I-5 freeway and, once on I-5, I thought I was doing pretty well. I knew that drunk people like to speed, so I kept my speed between 20 and 30 mph so the cops wouldn't notice me. Yeah right. I also tried to keep my driver's side tires on the turtles separating the lanes, so I could tell if I was swerving or not. There wasn't much traffic, so it didn't seem important that I was using more than one lane. A couple times I had to use all three lanes, but hardly ever.

Suddenly red and blue lights flashed in my rearview mirror and a siren wailed. Uh oh! I pulled over and waited while the officer marched up to my car. He shined his light in my eyes and pulled out his alcohol-breath tester. Of course I failed.

Seeing that half my body is paralyzed and that I don't look like I'm a danger to anyone, he didn't handcuff me when he put me in the back of his car. On our way to the Seattle Cop Shop, he pulled over another drunk driver.

When he went up to talk to the other drunk driver, he of course left me in the back seat of his squad car. I'd been drinking all night, what am I wanting to do? Exactly! I needed to let some water out. Since I hadn't been handcuffed, I didn't have to wet myself, I was able to make a nice little puddle on the floor.

Pretty soon the cop and the other drunk driver walk to the patrol car. The cop opens the back door on the other side of the car and tells the other drunk to get in. He got in. Almost immediately:

"S- - t! What the…"

I spent two nights and three days in jail. They put me in the same cell as red uniformed felons. I saw at least two fights. I didn't see any weapons, but these guys were beating the stuffing out of each other.

There was blood and broken teeth and handfuls of hair. I was freaking out. How'd I get in here? I haven't done any drunk driving since.

Stand-up comedy gave me plenty of opportunities to receive free drinks, but doing stand-up comedy also gives me plenty of reasons to stay clean and sober. Comedy routines require all that I have to give and I function at a much higher level if I keep my head clear, which is why I've returned to AA. I sometimes miss drinking, but except for a temporary feeling of exhilaration, there is really nothing good that drinking ever did for me.

Then why did I drink? Drinking blotted out reality and made me feel like I had control, among other things. Drinking gave me a sense of power. However, it turned out to be the power to destroy every aspect of my life—social, financial, physical, academic, not to mention my car. I remember one time when my friend, Joe, and I—whom Cheryl and I had gone with to the Bruce Springsteen concert—went out drinking.

As usual I drank way too much and when I went to the restroom, ended up falling and cracking open my forehead on the tile floor. That's one example of drinking causing me social embarrassment and physical pain, although the pain didn't come till the next day. I can't remember all the events that got me to AA, but I'm glad I made it.

Some people don't make it. AA tells new people to come to ninety meetings in ninety days. I figured if ninety in ninety is good, 300 in ninety would be even better.

The beauty of AA was that the worse I acted, the more people who had been around a while would nod their heads and say, "Keep coming back." Now I sponsor people and get to encourage newcomers to "Keep coming back." AA is a great program and I, and a lot of other lucky folks, owe AA credit for our happy and fulfilled lives. Thanks for everything, AA.

Another organization that helped me was a single's group that meets near my condo. They had a talent show in the summer of 1995. I wanted to be in it, but I didn't have any talent. I wondered, "What can I do to be in this talent show?" I know, I'll tell some jokes. Everybody likes to laugh.

The day came, and I got on stage and told some jokes. They were probably pretty lame (get it?). But people laughed and afterwards a girl came up to me and told me she was a former comedian and she said I had a "great stage persona" (Whatever that means). She didn't say she liked my jokes, but she took me to downtown Seattle to an open mic and I began doing stand-up comedy.

Over the years, projecting my voice into the microphone has improved my speech and increased my confidence. After doing comedy all over the Pacific Northwest, I started sharing my story in schools, elementary through university. I love doing stand-up comedy, and I'll always do it, but it's not nearly as fulfilling as inspirational speaking at school assemblies and before corporate or government audiences.

Even though I won first prize in the 2000 Laff-Off at Giggles Comedy Club in Seattle, I didn't feel like I had enough skill and comedic determination to make a career out of comedy. Actually, even if I did, some things I share just are not meant to be laughed at. Standup comedy is a tool I'm glad I experienced, but it was more a means to and end than an end in itself. My purpose is more fulfilled by focusing my energy and attention on delivering inspirational and motivational presentations that contain humor but that also have value people can actually use.

Organizing and delivering humorous talks for schools, businesses and other organizations has done a lot to forward my social and business skills. AA taught me to claim progress not perfection, and I'm being blessed with some incredible progress.

Becoming better at interacting with others is a lot like doing stand-up comedy and mainlining heroin. The more you do it, the better you get (I'm kidding). I never did heroin. I'm brain damaged, not retarded.

Actually, to retard something means to slow it down. I have definitely been slowed down, so maybe I am.

The human spirit is an amazing thing. It is capable of doing and becoming more than I ever recognized or expected. The fact is that we never really know our limits in life until we are pushed into them or until we push ourselves beyond what we are currently doing, and in my case, often pushing my limits in a harmful way.

It was so easy for me to just keep doing the same old-same ole. It's so easy to get caught up in a routine day after day where we do exactly what we already know how to do and don't push ourselves to go beyond that. And we typically will continue on that path until life throws us a curve ball that forces us to step up, or until we finally reach a point of misery where we decide enough is enough and we force ourselves to change our lives by going outside our comfort zone.

So often in life I thought to myself, "I could never handle that," but when push comes to shove and we have no choice but to handle it, it is amazing that somehow we do handle it. Our outer-limits of what we can handle are well beyond what we seem to think. We are stronger and more capable then we typically believe we are, so it's really a shame that it takes the negative trials to show us our true strength. Wouldn't it be so much better if we could push ourselves beyond our own limits without waiting for circumstances to force us there?

We all have the desire to push ourselves beyond our comfort zones as well as the desire to push ourselves to be more and do more than we are currently doing. Below is a daily checklist I have found helpful to make that happen:

Every morning when I wake up:

- I choose to do more and be more than yesterday,

- I don't allow any excuses to hold me back from making progress today

- No more procrastinating – START NOW!

Don't listen to negative talk. Remember, we don't know our limits, unless we test them. If we don't know our limits, how can anyone else?

No matter what we want to achieve, we're going to eventually reach our limits, limit out so to speak. We just need to make sure we're taking the necessary actions to make sure our limits don't limit our potential. Here are several things I do that help me push past my limits:

Find someone to help push me: Just that little bit of support encouraging us to keep going in the face of resistance can mean so much. Having someone on your side, on your team, can counter-balance the negative thinking we might have. Special people inspiring us can give us the courage to push past our comfort zones.

Take on a little more than you think you can: Pushing past our limits means taking on newer, progressively harder challenges. If we're not challenging ourselves to do bigger and better things on a regular basis, we're only working within the confines of what we can already do. That's a sure-fire way to stay exactly where we are and make little to no progress.

Imagine reaching your next level: Working on our dreams or goals can take a lot of focus. Where we put that focus matters a lot. We might know where we are and where we were, but are we where we want to be? Imagine being on the next level of reaching your dreams and take steps to get there.

Look at how others reached where we want to go: Whatever our goals are, there are probably others who have had them and succeeded in reaching them. We can look to them for inspiration as well as clues on what they did to push past their limits on their way to success.

Inspire ourselves to action: Find something that inspires us to reach our goals. Whether it is a video, quote or thought that inspires us to succeed, it should be something that fills us with passion and drives us to get things done. Inspiration is a powerful motivational tool.

Plan to succeed: Since half my body is paralyzed, the muscles that still work need to work at an optimal level. I have a personal trainer created workout routine. Planning for success means I get qualified advice from qualified people. I've worked on this book for endless hours getting the messages just the way I want them to be. I planned to write this book by doing tons of research and taking lots of writing classes and seminars.

Turning weaknesses to Strengths: Where there are weaknesses, there are limits. Think about a marathon runner. They won't be able to train very well for a marathon if they can't find a good running stride or have bad nutrition. These are big areas of weakness that makes training harder. Without correction, our weaknesses limit how far we can take ourselves.

Breaking down our Barriers: In order to reach our dreams or goals, we have to push through our limits and past our comfort zone. There are no shortcuts. Whatever is worth doing is worth doing well. That's been my personal motto for success in life. It's my way of reminding me to constantly push myself and not settle for average.

When facing our limits, the resistance we feel can be hard to overcome. But just by pushing ourselves a little harder, we really can accomplish so much more. Looking back, I remember the tough parts of rehab, but I also realize that doing it wasn't as bad as I imagined something like it would be. Our imaginations are fear factories that manufacture limits. And remember, I'm talking from a mountain of experience at overcoming obstacles that required years of rehabilitation. Don't let imagined limits stop you from doing anything. Just do it!

Is your life a series of challenges or a series of calamities? Do you see only limitations or do you also see possibilities? It's your choice. Your choices have the power to make you who you want to be, but they also have the power to keep you from becoming the person you were meant be. In other words, your choices can make you or break you. It's your choice. Be patient. As a Chinese proverb says, "The person who removes a mountain begins by carrying away small stones."

We have control of determining how much we will push our own limits in order to truly achieve our greatest potential in life. Don't sit passively by waiting for life events to force you to go beyond your limits, or provide an easier path. Do it yourself! It is empowering and gratifying to take charge and make it happen on your own. Push your limits! Discover the joy of living without regrets because you know you did your best!

Each one of us carries ingrained, unconscious ideas of just how happy and successful we can be. We can expand our potential for happiness and abundance in extraordinary ways by pushing past our limits. Believing you have limits is all that's stopping you from reaching your goals and dreams. Achieve NO LIMITS!

CHAPTER 31

My Take Away Thoughts

My trust in a higher power that wants me to survive and have love in my life is what keeps me moving forward.
--Kenny Loggins, Musician

You have only always to do what is right. It will become easier by practice, and you enjoy in the midst of your trials the pleasure of an approving conscience.
--Robert E. Lee (1807-1870, General

Live life to the fullest, and focus on the positive.
--Matt Cameron, Musician

PEOPLE'S SEARCH FOR A HIGHER POWER plays a central role for people overcoming great challenges. I do not want to limit the people *Achieving No Limits-Embracing Change* can help, so I won't say that one higher power is more valid than another. Not everyone needs to define their Higher Power.

For many, "knowing" is not an issue – the important thing is to understand we're not alone. Their Higher Power is an unseen and indescribable force that is the very sustenance of life. When we struggle, it's a shoulder to lean on, which gives us strength – our Higher Power is unconditional support. When we feel on top of the world, it keeps us in check – our Higher Power is the baseline between extremes; it's balance. Whether it's Nature, humanity, music, the universe, a little of each, or something else entirely, to many, belief in a Higher Power is about getting out of ourselves and knowing that it's okay to need help.

It's just a matter of letting go of our control, especially when we start to fall. Faith gives us personal resolve to get back up on our feet. Some may not know exactly what their Higher Power is, but it's clearly defined in their lives. Through their actions and words, and the way they interact with the world, their lives are a testament to its Truth. In other words, by defying explanation, their Higher Power has a strange way of giving meaning to all their questions – yet the answer is not what they seek. It's faith in knowing that when they're lost, their Higher Power is the direction, which points them toward salvation, which different people define differently.

I can't even truthfully say that having a Higher Power is absolutely necessary in overcoming challenging changes. All I can say with absolute certainty is that having a Higher Power has certainly helped me.

A concept of a Higher Power that is in the 4th edition of the AA Big Book is that of a Native American woman who said she found the Power greater than herself to be "the magic above the heads of the people in the meetings. I choose to call that magic 'Great Spirit.'"

If that's what freed her from the obsession to drink, my experience has to accept it as her experience. Everyone is my teacher. Some teach me what to do, some teach me what not to do. I am but a humble student, some may say '*grasshopper*'.

Unless a person specifically asks or gives some other reason for us to believe that they're open to such a conversation, most people's political views and spiritual beliefs are off limits as far as friendly conversation topics. You may seem to win an argument based on superior knowledge, but usually you will have gained neither a friend nor a convert to your way of thinking.

Irrespective of what religious beliefs one may have, there is usually at least one Source that is perceived to be the Ultimate Source, the Beginning of everything, the One holding everything together. The Ultimate Source may be perceived as God, Goddess, The Universe, Jesus, Buddha, other "Ascended Masters." We humans, *and* other living creatures, are beneath this Ultimate Source. We're unique, but connected as brothers and sisters through equality.

Challenges for People with Disabilities: People with disabilities face hostility more than you might imagine. My simply having disability parking privileges resulted in a clueless thug-like individual screaming at me about "bloody benefit scroungers" followed by additional insults. Few people with disabilities will be surprised.

The sad reality is that this kind of behavior happens more than many people realize. Because I am occasionally clueless, I just ignore it. And I've been known to educate my friends of how inappropriate it is to take a disability parking space.

It remains hard for people with a disability to find work, the place of perhaps greatest social integration, a place that would be healing and empowering for people with disabilities. One associate of mine sent 100 job applications revealing he was blind and he received no replies. Yet when he deleted this single fact, he was invited to 73 interviews. Hmm, equality?

People with disabilities are still seeking more equality in the work force and face unique challenges. While many employers hire people of all abilities, some can still not imagine a person with a disability fulfilling job requirements. Some people set limits on those with disabilities, keeping them from the jobs of their dreams.

Stereotypes (like people with disabilities) are often tougher barriers to break down than sidewalk curbs. Barriers within our public social support structure keep people with disabilities from seeking employment. Social barriers are perhaps the hardest to overcome. Most people have social groups at work and in their personal lives. In these groups, connections are made, jobs are offered, advice is shared and sometimes romance blooms. Becoming part of a group requires an invitation and a welcoming atmosphere. Many groups have yet to welcome any person with a disability.

There are not Victims, Only Choices: Contrary to popular belief, *there are no victims in this world* – only participants. We can't always control your circumstances, but we can control how we respond to them. And everyone has the power to *embrace change* at any time. It's still a concept difficult to accept, but we all create our own reality, from health to disease, happiness to sorrow and birth to death.

There are no "right or wrong" choices. They are just choices and our life experience can be no other way than how we design it to be. We are the orchestrator, architect and designer all combined into one. Our thoughts are pure energy translating every frequency into an experience. Do you think our thoughts end after they leave our heart and mind? They never end. If anything they will go out into the universe and come back at us like a boomerang.

All thoughts are creative and attract the energy that they emit. Love will attract love and fear will attract fear, but the greatest masters that have ever walked the Earth are those who have loved unconditionally in every moment of their lives.

> ## CHOICES
> Some people sit - some people try.
>
> Some people laugh - some people cry.
>
> Some people will - some people won't.
>
> Some people do - some people don't.
>
> Some people believe and develop a plan.
>
> Some people doubt - never think that they can.
>
> Some people face hurdles and give it their best.
>
> Some people back down when faced with a test.
>
> Some people complain of their miserable lot.
>
> Some people are thankful for all that they have got.
>
> And when it's all over - when it comes to an end —
>
> Some people lose out and some people win.
>
> We all have a choice - we all have a say.

Why Change is Always Scary and How to Embrace Change: Change is never easy, but more often than not, things change for the better. Whether it's changing your personal image, adapting to a new lifestyle or accepting something you are unfamiliar with, change is good once in a while.

Change is part of everyday life and yet some people find change challenging. If facing new situations fills us with dread, we can help ourselves by learning how to embrace change. Think about it, change is inevitable. At this very moment, for instance, our body and cells are changing. The earth, economy, technology, how we do business, and even how we communicate are changing. We can choose to resist the changes that are always afoot and ultimately be swept away by them. Alternatively, we could choose to cooperate with change, adapt to change, and benefit from change all the while stepping into greater levels of our prosperity.

Understand that it's natural to have a deep rooted fear of change. Change, of any type or through any stage in life, is often looked upon as frightening. If, however, change is embraced with a positive attitude, it becomes an opportunity to live with greater excitement and fulfillment.

So how do we actually embrace change? It's actually pretty easy – it begins by accepting that life is a journey of discovery and that change is part of that journey.

Most people know this, yet change is often resisted. Why? The reason is simple: once someone has become comfortable with the way things work (Status Quo), they naturally find it hard to embrace something different (Foreign Element). Doing so would mean they instantly become less competent, effective and efficient.

Most people know this, yet change is often resisted. Why? Again, the reason is simple: once someone has become comfortable with the way things work (Status Quo), they naturally find it hard to embrace something different (Foreign Element). Doing so, would mean they instantly become less competent, effective and efficient.

In today's world and globalized marketplace, being less is scary. It's drilled into us as children. We must be better than our peers-faster-higher-stronger. We think that only by being more than next guy is can we get ahead in life.

This is why change is always scary. Yet, it is the *Secret to Success*. Embrace change. Override our first instinctive reaction to run the other way. Adopt an open mind. Look at the change not as a threat to our current situation, but as an opportunity to learn and grow.

Often time, our habitual internal thoughts and dialogue stop us from living fully. In order to have a perspective that will serve us rather than hinder us, we must get rid of negative, limiting thoughts.

Once we are aware and mindful of our limiting thoughts, we can correct them and start embracing the changes in our life with greater positivism.

Remember, as we think, we travel, as we love, we attract, where we are today is because your thoughts brought us, where we will be tomorrow is where our thoughts brought us; see, a thought can do us more good than a doctor or a banker or a faithful friend, but it can also do us more harm than a brick. However, if we find it is really difficult to change our thoughts from negative to positive, and then we need to ask our understanding of God for help, He will help us if we try, and we can if we think we can.

You are an empowered individual, you always have choices, you are the captain and you are in your life's driving seat, so don't give your power away to someone else or some situation.

Thus, if you want to be happy or your life to improve in one way or another, don't expect things to radically change, unless you do something about it. If you keep doing things in the same way you have done, expect the same results.

If you continue to cruise along the same highway, expect it to lead you exactly where it has always led. To change your life for the better, you have to introduce a Foreign Element, trigger or change agent, shake things up, do things differently, adopt an improved mindset and be a different person. Your life depends on it.

Start embracing change today. Start living! Once you get things started, you will find change is full of amazing opportunities.

Accept the change. Everybody will experience change at least once in their life, and whether they are happy with this change or not, they will have to learn to adjust somehow, but this takes time.

Be patient. Change can be scary, but given some time, you will adjust to the new situation. This is dependent on the individual, but friends and family can help you to adjust.

Think about the positives. Change is normally for the better, like moving to a new house or school. While it may seem daunting at first, you will be able to see the positive aspects of being somewhere new or doing new things.

Talk to somebody. There is nothing worse than going through change and feeling like you have no-one to talk with. For instance, when going through puberty, a lot of things change. If you feel scared or upset by this change, talk to somebody you trust and explain to them what is making you uncomfortable or upset.

Think about how the difference will affect you. When change happens, people tend not to think too much about this change will affect them in the long run. Sit back for a moment and think about how much better things will be and stay positive about the change.

We Are Limitless: Once our amazing brains discover how it has learned to limit itself, it knows just how to readjust itself. As the brain network comes on line in the manner it's meant to exist in, no part of our life remains unaffected. As our emotions stabilize and our mental acuity picks up, our health and physical wellbeing advance also. Gone is our insecurity, our anxiety, our anger. Gone is our inexplicable sadness, depression, and thoughts of helplessness. Gone is our dependence on alcohol or mind-altering drugs. Life no longer feels as if we are stepping on the gas while someone else is stepping on the brake. In fact, with optimized use of our brain, we optimize our entire life. We can at last be the limitless individuals we were born to be.

When life gives you a hundred reasons to cry, show life you have a thousand reasons to smile.

MEET AL FOXX

Founder & President of
Winners Don't Quit Association

Inspirational Humorist, Comic & Author of
"Achieving NO LIMITS—Embracing Change"

Trauma survivor Al Foxx has had over 18-years of experience as a professional speaker and entertainer, with demonstrated ability to make people laugh, cry and think. Al Author of *NO LIMITS* (published 2008); and *Achieving NO LIMITS-Embracing Change* (published in 2014).

Al Foxx is the founder of Winners Don't Quit Association (www.WinnersDontQuit.com), a non-profit which has been in place since 1998. Al's mission is to help people with and without disabilities to embrace change by:

1. Inspiring them to believe in their own possibilities.

2. Enabling individuals, both disabled and non-disabled, to better understand one another.

Al Foxx offers a glimpes of the world few people take the time to notice. By looking at life through the eyes of a person with physical disabilities, Al inspires us to turn tragedy into triumph, and write a happy ending to the book of our lives.

Al reminds us that people with disabilities are much tougher than you think. He recommends warmly and respectfully approaching individuals with disabilities and to not be afraid of offending someone, *believing you may say something wrong.* Isolation hurts more than saying the wrong thing.

"People with disabilities are tough and have heard it all. There is nothing you can say that hasn't been said before, so take a chance!" Isolation is one of the biggest issues for people with disabilities and this can be avoided.

We all have disabilities of one kind or another; some are visible, and some are invisible. I want to help people know there is hope out there for all of us.

"People are struggling with a variety of life's challenges. Learning new skills to better cope with ongoing changes includes acceptance of reality, flexibility and adaptability. These skills will always be an asset throughout your life."

As a person with disabilities for over 34 years, Al knows what it means to have to completely change your life, and not by choice.

Al Foxx loved his Yamaha 650 Special. At 18, he felt invincible. His powerful bike carried him down country roads and weaved between cars on busy city streets.

One spring day in May of 1980, Al lost track of time while spending time with his fiancé. Suddenly, realizing he was late to meet his buddies at a rock concert, Al hopped on his bike and gunned out of the driveway.

He knew he should slow down, but he kept speeding up. Al never saw the truck that came out from a side street, through the stop sign. His speeding bike slammed into the truck and stopped dead. He flew over the handlebar--his helmet and face bones breaking against the side of the truck. Al suffered a massive traumatic brain injury that left him completely incapacitated. A tar-roofer by trade, Al's world collapsed when doctors told him he would never walk, talk or drive again.

What doctors didn't anticipate was the strength of Al's spirit. Unwilling to accept the gloomy prognosis, Al set out to bring himself back to as much functionality as was possible. Focusing on the winning-at-life formulas learned from his years with rehab psychotherapists, and other rehabilitation training, Al now shares these valuable lessons with other people facing challenges with big changes. Motorcycle crashes come in all shapes and sizes; divorce, bankruptcy, loss of a loved one, loss of a job, scary medical concerns, to name a few. While sharing these lessons, Al realized his humorous story-telling presentations were helping people; and helping people made Al feel good.

Although he was told he would never walk without a cane, talk understandably or drive legally, he drives to his local gigs, he limps onto stages throughout the United States and in Canada, and has spoken to hundreds of audiences. He does all of those things differently than he did before, but he has brought himself to a post-trauma identity based on what he can be, do and connect with.

Instead of working as a tar-roofer he has become a humorist, author, and an inspirational speaker. From an amateur night at a church function, Al Foxx started his speaking career at Seattle's Comedy

Underground in 1995 and focused on learning the craft of stand-up comedy, opening for many top comedians. Competing with other feature acts, Al won the Giggles Laff-Off Comedy contest in 2000. Shortly after that, Al began his speaking career.

His motto, "Winners focus on what they have, not what they don't have," acts as a great reminder that we all have a choice about where we place our focus. Our focus determines our future. And as Bill Cosby says, *"Through humor, you can soften some of the worst blows that life delivers. And once you find laughter, and no matter how painful your situation might be, you can survive it."*

COMEDY CLUB PHOTOS

Each week THE COMEDY UNDERGROUND presents open mic for professional and amateur comedians to test new material and to develop their acts. Soon Al Foxx became a favorite!

Al won the Giggles Laff-Off Comedy contest in 2000. Giggles Comedy Club was a comedy club located in Seattle's University District and consistently brought in some of countries top comedians.

In all professional presentations, Al includes his skills learned on the comedy circuit. So, if you choose to book Al, you can count on laughing a lot! Regardless of the serious message he presents about a variety of subjects, he has learned to find the humor in serious situations! And as Andrew Carnegie says, *"There is little success where there is little laughter."*

BOOK AL FOXX

TO SPEAK AT YOUR NEXT EVENT

If you could have an inspirational and humorous, industry specific customized presentation about embracing change by accepting the book you've been given, choosing to write a happy ending and caring about others, what value would that have for your organization?

Al Foxx is an inspirational and humorous professional speaker and author of "Achieving NO LIMITS-Embrace Change." He has delighted audiences all across the country for over 15 years with his authentic and humorous presentations. His love of speaking began at amateur talent night at a church function. Shortly after that, Al Foxx officially began his comedy career at Seattle's Comedy Underground. Several years later, he became an award winning comic by winning the Giggles Comedy Club Laff-Off (Seattle) in 2000.

Today he drives to his local speaking engagements, limps onto the stage, and gets paid to share his humorous insights with people who begin to see their own situations and challenges in a new light. Suddenly, they can believe that there is hope in their own possibilities. As a speaker and entertainer, Al appeals to audiences of all ages: from Fortune 500 companies to universities, government agencies, churches and schools.

Go to Al's website (see below) to find testimonials, audio and written, as well as YouTube videos and radio shows that will help you decide if Al's is a good fit for your organization.

(425) 820-0367 – Booking Manager
www.WinnersDontQuitAssociation.com
www.WinnersDontQuit.com
www.AttitudeMan.com

Al Foxx on stage—State of Washington Brain Damage Association

Al Foxx on stage—Gilford College in Greensboro, North Carolina

Al Foxx on stage—Annual HUG Conference
Seattle Fairmont Olympic Hotel, Seattle, WA

Book Sales Table—Annual HUG Conference
Fairmont Olympic Hotel, Seattle, WA

Al Foxx on stage—Annual HUG Conference
Seattle Fairmont Olympic Hotel, Seattle, WA

Speaker Testimonials

"Al Foxx is a powerful, courageous and honest speaker who takes you through an incredible and inspiring journey of self-discovery and leaves you with a feeling of gratitude and self-awareness. "

Shirin Sherkat, Psy.D.,
Parent Strategist, Author of *"Create Happy Kids"*
www.createhappykids.com

"Al Foxx has one of the most unique stories I have ever heard. He will make you laugh, cry and think. If you get a chance to hear him speak (or read his books), stop what you are doing and run to sign up. You will thank me."

Mark Matteson
Best-Selling Author of *Freedom from Fear*
www.sparkingsuccess.net/

"Al Foxx had me in tears--both because I was so inspired by him, his story and the way he tells it--and because he is hilarious! Al reminded me of something that is very powerful: you can't judge a book by its cover because when you do, you miss out on the PURE GOLD within. Al is pure gold--and has a heart and courage to match. I whole-heartedly recommend Al as a powerful speaker, motivator, and inspired man who lights a fire under your "But..." and melts your heart at the same time! Bravo!"

Kris Prochaska, MA, LMHC
Guide to Confident Communication-Heart & Soul Speaking
www.speakfreelynow.com

"The response by all levels of the several hundred staff in attendance was overwhelming! The content of your message was matched by the way in which it was delivered. For many years in our County, we have

been trying to point out that "I am not my disability". Your presence in our community put the exclamation point on that concept."

Michael McCartan,
Executive Director, St. Clair County Community Mental Health
<u>www.scccmh.org/</u>

"Mr. Al Foxx was the keynote speaker at the annual spring HUG conference in Seattle. HUG (Healthcare User Group) is made up of Health Payors from all over the United States. Al's presentation was extremely motivating, inspirational, humorous, and most importantly touched the hearts of those in attendance. Al stayed to sign his book and talk with each one on an individual basis. As President of the HUG Board, I was lucky enough to have many come up to me and thank me for inviting Al to be our guest speaker. Honestly, I was the lucky one—I was able to attend the keynote speech given by Al."

Denny Kinkead
President of HUG Board
<u>www.sparkingsuccess.net/</u>

"Al Foxx changed my perspective on a couple elements of life - with his humor, insights and down-to-earth style. He lifts you up into new places, from which you smile - or guffaw, seeing a broader view. His humor, stage presence, physicality and powerful personal story quickly captivate - and I wholeheartedly believe he will skillfully pluck will at your heart strings."

Marilyn Schoeman
Author of *GO!*
How to Think, Speak and ACT to Make Good Things Happen
<u>http://www.gogreenlightway.com</u>

I recently saw Al speak at a conference in Seattle on Embracing Change. Al has a great and import message, not only for people with disabilities, but for all of us. He shows us not only by his words but his own stories that no matter what difficulties or tragedies we experience, we can come back stronger, capable and even happier. Al's delivery is very effective but the added bonus is that he's funny too. Imagine that, using humor to deal with and encourage others who are affected by tragedy. I would highly recommend Al's work and message to everyone.

Mike Manor
President of Midnight Mouse Productions

I would give Al a very strong recommendation. He was especially inspiring to the teenagers and very appropriate. My 16 year old son said Al brought tears to his eyes. We should have had him speak longer. He was great. The audience loved him and told me many times how much they enjoyed his talk.

Carrie Harris
Education Service Center
Duvall High School Bachelorette

34707519R00152

Made in the USA
Charleston, SC
13 October 2014